A Sky Goddess! Who...Me???

The Amazing Travel Adventures of Alice in Wanderlust

BY

Paige Becquet
(aka Alice Miller)

Mosaic Design
Book Publishers

A Sky Goddess! Who...Me???

The Amazing Travel Adventures of Alice in Wanderlust

First Printing – January 2017
Second Printing – April 2017

ISBN: 978-0-9968933-4-3 *(paperback)*

Printed in the United States of America on acid-free paper.

Published by Mosaic Design Book Publishers
Dearborn, Michigan USA

0 1 2 3 4 5 6 7 8 9

"When once you have tasted flight,
you will forever walk the earth
with your eyes turned skyward,
for there you have been, and there
you always long to return."

Leonardo Da Vinci

DEDICATION

This book is dedicated to my father, Dr. Joseph Miller, who handed down to me his quest for the unknown. While my forté may be in cultural exploration, his was in inventing medical cures. My dad was a pediatrician, but over time he developed terrible allergy problems, and

realized that it would not make sense to travel outside of Mobile, Alabama just to get treatment from an allergy specialist. No, it seemed to make more sense to simply add the skill to his practice and become an allergist in his own right so he could cure himself!

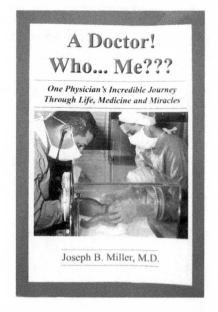

Against all odds, my dad became the *first* allergist in Alabama.

He was very successful and even discovered many cures, one being Aleviare®, an aerosol therapy to liquefy viscid secretions in bronchopulmonary disease, clearing the mucus in clogged nasal membranes. His work resulted in saving the lives of thousands of babies. He was even honored by the mayor of Mobile who announced a 'Dr. Miller Day,' complete with a parade down Government Street!

Forever accepting new challenges, my father did the same with other unusual undertakings, like learning karate. Interested in martial arts, he drove countless hours to New Orleans to take lessons. He finally brought the instructor, T. Mikami of the Japan Shotokan Karate Association, to Mobile and opened a dojo with him. Setting another 'first,' my father became the first black belt in Alabama. I can't help but remember that Frank Sinatra was one of his favorite singers. After all, what would Frank have said about him? He did it *his* way, of course!

So you could say that I'm following in my father's footsteps, and writing about my life's escapades, just as he so often encouraged me to do. He would tell me that by listening to my adventures and putting himself mentally in my shoes, he felt he was living a second life. However, I have to admit, I did not get a black belt in Japanese-style karate, like he did! My black belt was in American style!

As the Mad Hatter said in *Alice in Wonderland*, "The apple doesn't fall far from the tree." I'm convinced that my free spirit and my drive to *discover and conquer* were definitely inherited. My father always taught me to hold my head high if I walk through a storm and to always go for the gold.

He was such a laid back, soft-spoken man. Never in my entire life did he lose his temper, except when I told him I was going to be a stewardess. My mother said, "Don't worry Joe. She'll do that for a year and then become a school teacher."

I was named after Alice in Wonderland by my father. However, I didn't really feel like the sweet, innocent Disney character, so at 14-years-old, I changed my name to Paige. "Paige the Rage" became my nickname in my karate school and it felt more like me. My mother thought it was a joke, but when she saw that I stuck with it, she went to the courthouse and made it legal (as my 21st birthday present) as my middle name.

Now as an adult, after re-reading the stories of her, she seems like a really curious and cool chick. She had amazing travel adventures just like I do. So I'm honored to have her name. *{For a little Alice fun in reading my story, don't be surprised if you find yourself in the pages of her magical tale of fantasy by Lewis Carroll. Watch for these brackets.}*

Although I have always enjoyed the companionship of traveling with friends, the events that warm my heart and bring goosebumps to my skin happened when I was alone. I enjoyed playing things by ear, hanging out with the locals, breaking down barriers, and getting into the heartbeat of the culture. I loved discovering new religions, clothing, music, and taboos. But most of these adventures never could have turned out the way they did if I had had a companion. And writing a book would have been impossible. Alone, I could let my brain be creative and I could leave myself open to any spur-of-the-moment happenings.

So, this is what I recommend: plan your vacation with friends, get excited together while researching, and enjoy your time together, but arrange to get more time off than the others. That way, you can stay and 'smell the roses' with your new local friends! As such, you are not talking absentmindedly, taking tons of pictures of each other, and consequently missing all the enchantment that surrounds you. You are free to be spontaneous to new, enlightening, educational, and sometimes extraordinary experiences. You can just go and do whatever your instincts tell you to do, without your friend, spouse, or tour leader saying it can't or shouldn't be done!

Then, like Sinatra, you too can say, 'I did it *My Way*'!

Dedicated to Mom

When I was five, my sister, Joan, and I were playing a silly game. She would drop bobby pins down a hole in a pink doll-baby bassinet. The hole was actually a drain to let the water out after bathing the doll. I was lying on the floor with the tube in my mouth blowing the bobby pins up as they came down. The point was to see how far up I could blow the pins into the air. One got caught in my throat and cut off my air supply. I started turning blue. I couldn't breathe! Joan pulled me up and ran into the living room where mom was talking to a man about insurance. Joan told her what had happened. Mom turned me upside down and started whacking me on the back. The pin came out of my mouth and I was saved. (Hey, thanks Mom!)

Who knew this was the preface to my whole life of dangerous and life-threatening experiences, as you will soon read! Meanwhile, Mom became overprotective of my activities (even with simple slumber parties at the home of one of my best friends, Sandra). Mom was afraid I had inherited the *wild hair* of my father: to dream the impossible

Me and my sister Joan (right)

dream, to climb the highest mountain no matter what the obstacles! She became so strict that I felt trapped. This brought on the feeling of rebellion ODD (oppositional defiance disorder). I started feeling that I wanted to do exactly what she told me *NOT* to do and to break all the rules! Therefore, I guess I turned into a rebel. Really? Who me?

I wanted to do everything and go everywhere, so becoming a stewardess was the perfect occupation. Mom made me become the Christopher Columbus of the family to explore new territories and new frontiers and meet new people who enhanced my life's journey. Observing her, I captured an amazing gift: learning how to organize my life. By noting her skills, I kept diaries in my calendars and documented everything with pictures. I have recently been digging up my many organized albums and files, and I know, without all this information, this book could not exist.

In summary, my mom gave me life, then she saved my life, and then she *spent her life* making sure I was safe!

INSPIRATION

I was inspired to write this book by my little cousin, Brad Young, the son of Beth and Alan, from Mobile. When he was in grammar school, he heard about my exciting journey in the Far East when I had bathed in a lake with elephants, among other outlandish adventures. He convinced me that I should keep a journal on my next trip so I could come to his school and talk about my travels at *Show and Tell*. Well, this is it! It is exactly as I scribbled it in a notebook 33 years ago.

So, it came to be that I would do anything to keep up this journal. Even when I was suffering from a near fatal illness in India, bedridden and full of gut wrenching pain, I had to keep up my notes in case I made it. Well, I survived to *Show and Tell* my story. For this book, I've added a few more of my global escapades to give you a glimpse of the tremendous, colorful, and crazy adventures I've had around the world. If you like it, tell Brad. It was all his idea!

"Not all those who wander are lost."
J.R.R. Tolkien

Here's my version of Tolkien's sentiments: Don't be afraid to *jump into the rabbit hole* like I did and find the unexpected!

I encourage young people to 'seize the moment.' Experience your dreams when you are young. When you are older, life will surely put obstacles in your way, whether they be financial, family, health, or any number of other things.

I don't hesitate to namedrop in my writings. I'll mention names of people and countries galore! Along the way, I've bonded with so many incredible folks around the world who, interestingly enough, are all interested in pretty much the same thing: world peace.

Grab hold to the wings of a dragonfly and live life to the fullest with no fear...

ACKNOWLEDGEMENTS

I would like to thank special people for encouraging me and helping me write this journey:

Jenny Quan

Joan McCracken

Diane Eaton

McPatti/Bruce Langston

Sherry Boyce

Larry Simpson

Susan Giffin

Georgia Brown

Carol Miller/Bruce Miller

Alain Becquet/Brigitte Becquet

Maury Gurwitch

Dylan Smith

Merle/Michelle Leroux

Bill Moore

Willie Tobin

Steve Ghannam

Mimi Dyer

June Cline

Senait Chrisostomo

Katey Scallion

CONTENTS

Part 2: Deeper Discoveries

INTRODUCTION

For many, being a stewardess is a very hard but wonderful profession. But I like to believe that I have taken it to a whole 'nother level, soaring to another dimension, if you will, and realizing a more adventurous vision.

I've always had an unquenchable curiosity to explore, a thirst to learn different languages and customs, and a hunger for cuisines from people who I would not have met ordinarily. So I've turned it into a lifestyle and an extraordinary passion like no other.

Unlike a lot of people I know, I love to escape 'life.' I love to leave behind the hustle and bustle of daily routines, paying bills, appointments with doctors, dentists, and chiropractors. As a stewardess, I took full advantage of my personal leave time to go on adventurous journeys for extended periods. Sometimes I would not return for several months, even up to six, in order to lather my brain with fresh air, clear my mental toxins and imbibe a unique and harmonious reality of existence. At the time of this writing, I've been to 120 countries in all seven continents. It's been extraordinary!

I hope my enthusiasm is transparent and rubs off on you a little bit. You'll notice my story-telling jumps around a bit, {like the white rabbit}, so I can share the most enchanting highlights of my travels with you. As far as I'm concerned, you are now entering my Magic Carpet Zone.

So buckle your seatbelt and enjoy the ride!

Part 1

MIRACLES
OF SURVIVAL

Chapter 1

"The more I traveled the more I realized that
fear makes strangers of people who should be friends."
Shirley MacLaine

Pakistan – Islamabad, Peshawar

Salaam Alaikum! (Peace be upon you!)

WHEW! I finally arrived at a destination that I have long wondered about, been intrigued by, and yet was terrified of. All I ever had heard, seen, or read about this part of the world scared the hell out of me and my two, courageous globetrotting companions, Linda and David. We really didn't know if we would make it back home alive, and, even better, all in one piece! In this part of the world, cutting off your hand could be punishment for stealing and it is not unheard of to acquire a fatal disease. We were definitely outside of our comfort zones.

Many of our friends asked us why we were taking such a huge risk to travel to an unsafe and unpredictable country like Pakistan. It was a very reasonable question, after all. But how do you answer a *'Why'* question like that? All I could do was recite Muhammad Ali's inspiring words:

"He who is not courageous enough to take risks
will accomplish nothing in life."

I think I've been living my life by that credo!

After disembarking in Islamabad, David tried to take the lead for the group. After all, the custom in these parts is to ignore the women and keep them quiet. We are the scum of the earth, of course. But, crazy as *hail* in summer, I threw caution to the wind, and started to head to the bank—to get some funds for our fun—without the protection of my male friend. However, I soon realized I was going to need a ride to get there. Being a pretty independent kind of girl, I turned to a man standing by, and with David less than ten feet away, I asked the man about getting a taxi.

David was frantic with fear, certain that I was going to get raped on the spot by such a bold move. But nothing happened. We got a taxi and were on our way.

Having completed our errands, the three of us checked into the Intercontinental Hotel. Now, believe me, snuggling into luxury accommodations is not my usual speed since I usually find that cheap guesthouses are warmer and more fun. But for this trip, we felt that we wanted to strike a balance in this third world country where you have to guard against filth. Besides, when you get a 50% airline discount and split it among three people, staying in a first class hotel is, well, a no-brainer.

For the rest of the day, the three of us swam in the hotel's huge pool, took naps, and went to the lively bazaar. To our astonishment, there were no hassles. We met Mujib and Muz Sahib, who invited us to enjoy some chai (tea) with them at a local teahouse where we listened to gorgeous sitar music from the musical artist, Ravi Shankar. We relaxed and told stories about our families in the U.S.A. and explained that we were three crew members from Delta Air Lines who shared the love of adventurous travel. I explained further that we were backpacking through Southeast Asia with the advantage of flying almost free due to our airline profession, which included substantial hotel discounts. I told my new friends that we wanted to do our hardest traveling now while we were still relatively young. I elaborated that, as we grow older, we seem to reach a point where we have to be led on tours and take cruises! They laughed hysterically.

After our morning flight to Peshawar, I referenced a list of contacts that I had received from my friend Muzaffar, who had given me the list for traveling in Pakistan. I had met him at a party in Atlanta, Georgia at the home of Yasser, the son-in-law of Pakistan's ex-President Bhutto, who had been hanged when East and West Pakistan divided, and Zia took over to form Bangladesh. Starting at the top of the list, we called Jewab and went to meet his family. We enjoyed kebab patties *(chapli kabob)* and various types of fruit indigenous to the area. They smoked the mango-flavored tobacco from a *hookah or chilom pipe*. Jewab took us to buy Pakistani rugs from Mushtar at the Bukhana House. Wishing to blend in with the local people, we went shopping for native attire called *Shalwar-Kameez*. These are loose and comfortable slacks and blouses that help stave off Pakistan's humidity.

I had another list, consisting of contacts in London that I had made when I did layovers there. On the list was Bayswater, a section of London, and I went there alone, on purpose. I had been told that the majority of people from Pakistan, India, Nepal, Burma, and Thailand lived there. So I simply made an excuse to start a conversation with people that 'looked the part.' After sharing 'a spot of tea' with many people who started out as strangers, I achieved my goal: to have a list of local contacts so I could avoid being the 'tourist' on my next trip!

CHAPTER 2

"If you reject the food, ignore the customs,
fear the religion, and avoid the people,
you might better stay at home."
James Michener

Pakistan – Rawalpindi, Swat

Our next flight was going to take us to Karachi, but there were so many Muslims returning from Mecca *(Hajj)* on that flight, that it was jammed. The airport manager saw our dilemma and suggested that we visit Swat, which is located just north of Peshawar. We followed his suggestion.

After a fantastic 'Paki' lunch at Dean's Hotel in Swat, we took a four-hour tour through the villages, while buffaloes and camels walked alongside us. By evening, we arrived at the night market and watched street chefs making *naan* (bread) in the underground oven. It smelled fantastic. We went shopping in Inam's Place for more Pakistani clothes and met the shop owner, Inam. He invited us to his beautiful home, where we met his family, and his wife sewed pockets into my Shalwar-Kameez to hide my money. Feeling safer and unburdened from having to carry a purse, it was very hand-y!

We were truly amazed at how nice and cordial Pakistani people could be. They were not evil or mean as we had heard; they were not

what we would have expected in our wildest dreams. The kids were adorable and always jumped at the chance to be in our photos. People in Pakistan are beautiful. They have dark gorgeous eyes, thick hair, bright white straight teeth, and beautiful smiles.

After a hurried breakfast with Inam, we went back to his shop and bargained for souvenirs. Midday, having only barely gained an appetite, we went for lunch at Inam's beautiful mansion. It included naan with kebab patties, mutton kebab, mango curry. Afterward, we drove all over Swat Valley and bought necklaces of lapis lazuli at an antique shop. We toured ancient ruins and met Mana Saif Al-Ajami, a Saudi Arabian sent by the prince of Saudi to buy a falcon for $50,000 from Pesharian Shahjehan, a falcon hunter.

Back at our hotel for the evening, our new friends ordered a humongous feast in their room and invited us over. They had spread a sheet out on the floor and all the food was laid out upon it. We were joined by Agha Ismali, who was a film producer of a movie called *Khyber Horse*, and we wolfed down an array of hot, spicy, delicious dishes.

Room service brought beer. When the porter asked, "Where should I put this?" Linda looked at him and pointed down her throat. "Right here," she said. Linda's sense of humor always kept us laughing.

Mana joined us and we played with his falcon. I slept with a pet lizard.

We met Nilofer, a jeweler, who took us to his shop. We bought gold, topaz, and lapis. We later went to a party with twins, Neseem and Nashrine, the princes of the royal family. It was in a plush house in Karachi with servants and chauffeurs. Every room was decorated luxuriously with velvet, silks, gold, and silver. Everything was over opulent. However, to our surprise, the bathroom had a hole in the floor instead of a toilet! (Some ancient customs still prevail.) Amazing!

Dinner was very classy and there was plenty of liquor, even though it had supposedly been banned in Pakistan due to the Islamic faith. (When you're with the royal family, anything goes!)

They all wore western clothes, but we Americans, of course, had on our Shalwar-Kamiz. They got a kick out of us wearing their traditional clothing to the party.

The next morning, Nilofer took us crabbing on the Arabian Sea. We threw nets out and scooped up the crabs from the waters. We rushed back to the airport to catch our flight to Delhi, but we were secretly hoping the flight would be full so that we'd have an excuse to stay in Pakistan with our new friends for a few days more. But we made the flight after all and continued our adventure.

Upon arriving in Delhi, we took a taxi to Jukaso Inn. Late in the evening, we went into the dark scary night, stopped at a sidewalk café, and ate betel nut leaf, or rather chewed and spit it out. It is supposed to get you to a higher plateau. Yuk! Horrible taste! I decided to stay on the plateau I was on!

We went to the tourist bureau to get our next itinerary, and on we went to Indian Airlines to have them write *three zillion tickets to everywhere*. This would give us 'open' tickets to many more cities without having to commit to a date. Such is the advantage of working for an airline: you just 'wing it' (pun intended).

Someone asked me if I was going to trek in Nepal when we got there. My answer, of course, was, "Yes! I'll trek all the way from the airport to the first taxi available!" While the group had made a pact not to buy anything that day, I broke the rules. *Who me?* I bought lapis and silver bracelets. I couldn't help myself! We went onto the Gandhi Memorial and saw where he had been cremated, or, as Linda put it: "where he made an ash out of himself."

So sari!

CHAPTER 3

"We travel, some of us forever.
To seek other places, other lives, other souls."
Anais Nin

Nepal, the Himalayas

Our journey continued to Kathmandu, Nepal, an ancient Himalayan kingdom where time has stopped and life has stood still. It has been closed to foreigners since 1952. Kathmandu has survived invasions by flower children and is now filled with serious trekkers. We had to dodge cows walking down the street as we walked to town. We watched the Newars (valley people) buying and selling their wares. Sherpas and the high hill people of Tibetan stock, called gurkhas, were everywhere. They are soldiers who march daily through Durbar Square and down the streets of Kathmandu. They are hailed as one of the best fighting forces in the world today and are known to carry the famous Kukri knife.

We toured the Baidyanath Temple, one of the world's largest Buddhist *stupas*, said to contain bones of the Buddha who preceded Gautama Buddha, and we joined in on the monks' music and prayer chanting. We continued to the Temple of the Living Goddess where the caste system selects a five-year-old girl to spend her entire life as a virgin in a temple alone. The selection process is based on throwing buffalo heads into a group of people. The girl showing the least fear becomes the goddess.

Bhaktapur, the village of the Newars people, was next on our tour. We joined in on their authentic folk dancing in the square and indulged in a huge feast of Nepalese dishes. The yogurt with coconut was amazing. *Aili*, tequila-like liquor made of rhododendron flowers, was served as well. Bhaktapur, which was founded about 900 A.D., looks like a museum with its fine sculpture, woodcarvings, art, and medieval architecture dedicated to many different gods and goddesses.

We decided to veer off to Durbar Square to what is called Freak Street. Guys came up to us, asking, "Hashish? Opium? Smack? Hash oil? Change money?" We thought about it for, well, not at all. Uh, I think *not*!

Meanwhile we walked through the neat village of Tamil and headed to the Monkey Temple where we enjoyed observing monks, chanting prayers, and playing music with horns, drums, and bells.

Royal Nepal Airlines took us to Tiger Tops to ride elephants in Chitwan National Park with Michele from Singapore. While we were riding on those magnificent animals, David dropped my camera. It must have been at some point between when we saw the rhino on the lake and when we walked through the thick jungle 30 minutes later, trekking through grass that was literally 'as high as an elephant's eye.' I thought it would be impossible to find the camera, but the elephant had keen eyesight and memory. It actually led the guides straight to the camera, so they could return it to me. Amazing! *"Hathi mera sathi"* (Elephant, my friend).

Meanwhile, someone yelled that a tiger *(bangebhale)* had taken the bait left for him on the cliff, so we all quickly scrambled into the jeeps and went to the Tiger Blind to go watch. We saw a male tiger chew on a buffalo carcass and finally break, crack, and yank off a lower rib before taking off into the brush. Then, with our awesome guides, we traveled by canoe down the River Narayani, and reached the tented camp. We saw a fantastic array of wildlife: herons, egrets, vultures, swallows, storks, and crocodiles.

After checking in at our cute little tented rooms, we ate a delicious Nepalese lunch while a guide sang us a song. Later, he wrote down the lyrics for me, as I love to always have a song in my pocket to practice when I am waiting for something such as a bus, train, plane, rickshaw, boat, motorcycle, or whatever. I have done this throughout my travels, and so far, I can sing a song in twenty languages.

After a quick and cold but refreshing swim in the river, David, my hero, rescued me from the current. You could say that he owed it to me, after all, for losing my camera while riding the elephants. David, I love you. *(Maya luk cha.)* Our guides took us through the jungle, where we searched for wildlife, but only found a spotted deer, tiger tracks, and rhino droppings. Oh well, *poop* happens!

We slept well by the rushing rapids of the lake in Dhulikhel, a countryside medieval town at a height of 5,000 feet, then rose early 5:00 a.m. to watch the sun rise over the Himalayas. No, not just your average

morning. The people there were friendly, darling people. There were many children carrying babies on their backs and women with as many as 15 earrings on one ear.

After spending an amazing day in the most incredible scenery, Linda and I wished David farewell as he was heading back to the United States. He was sad that he had not been able to get more vacation time, and that he'd have to miss our visit to the Taj Mahal!

Later that night, I joined my new friend Nirmal, whom I had met on our last flight. Following dinner, we took a motorcycle ride to Nagarkot, just in time to catch the sunset.

The day marked the start of the annual (as well as biggest and bloodiest) festival celebrating the triumph of good over evil. The festival was devoted to Durga, the goddess of battle, whose statue shows her holding weapons in ten hands. Along the street, everyone was walking their goats on the way to be slaughtered at Dakshinkali. I watched the slaughter, with blood squirting everywhere, and I couldn't help myself. I started to gag. But by the third goat, I got over it. It's amazing what you can get used to.

I celebrated Durga with a local couple, Penny and Pani. We enjoyed the specialty dinner of goat meat and rice while we sat on the floor and ate with our hands. Side dishes included goat's head and pickled fruit. We drank Tumba, a beer made of millet and rice fermented by adding hot water.

After dinner, Michele and I shopped for Tibetan tankas, which are Tibetan paintings on cotton or silk, portraying a Buddhist deity or scene. What originally was marked for sale for 160 rupees (about $12), we purchased for 120 rupees, by bargaining. These beautifully detailed cultural artifacts were designed to be displayed for short periods of time at religious gatherings and on monastery walls. They were treated very delicately and kept in dry places, rolled up to prevent moisture affects. Therefore, tankas last a long time and are used for personal meditation as well. The artistic detail displayed was so elaborate, depicting one central deity surrounded by other small figures.

Even today, tankas serve as more than just decoration; they also serve a very important purpose in Tibetan Buddhism. They are teaching tools that represent the life of Buddha, other deities, and other historic events. "The Wheel of Life" is one common, widely reproduced, visual representation of the Abhidharma teachings.

I was very impressed with the stories depicted by the tankas. I bought three for myself and four more to sell at home to museums! (Which I did for $400 apiece.)

Nirmal's friend picked us up on the motorcycle, and we rode over to his warehouse, which was full of carpets. Then, we enjoyed buttered and salted Tibetan tea with his mother and sister.

Later, we ventured to a local bar for rice beer called Chang, where we met a local singer, like Elvis Presley. We all sang together and made great harmony! We walked up the numerous steps to Pashupatinath, the most famous of all Hindu Shiva temples, where the deceased are brought to be cremated on the banks of the Bagmati River.

The Himalayas

When you're travelling, from time to time there comes a day when playing has to be put on the backburner to do business. Such was the case on this day. It was a big hassle getting our Indian Airline tickets rerouted to go to Varanasi along the way to Delhi. Everything had to be written because there weren't computers yet. Making matters worse, the agents stopped and closed for lunch right in the middle of the whole process and we had to sit and wait until they re-opened. What??? Were they serious?? Oh no! I guess that's how meditation became so popular in India. Another way to put it is this: when someone throws you a lemon, don't make lemonade. Remain calm and meditate, instead.

Eventually, the tickets were issued.

Then chaos ensued. We wanted to book a rafting tour so we ran all over the place to find tour agencies that would set it up for us. We soon learned that, due to the Dusai Festival, all the businesses had shut down for the day. Business after business was closed. Apparently, the staff did not even bother to come in to work. All in all, that part of our day was a total bust.

We gave up on the rafting tour for the time being, and I decided to view the Himalayas via a tour plane instead. I took a rickshaw for ten rupees to get tickets. When I reached the ticket office, people were pushing and shoving and hovering over my shoulder to be next in line. It was total chaos! Didn't anyone hear of a queue?

I tried to make a long distance call to my friend and fellow stewardess, Susan K., who was 'back at the ranch.' She was in charge of my schedule to help me take more time off. It took me an hour to make the call, compared to a second's click on today's cell phones. Again, lots of time was expended but totally wasted, as she wasn't home. I finally got the ticket for the tour, but by that time, I was mentally and physically exhausted and my back was aching badly. I thought, "Where is my chiropractor? I need an adjustment!" So I went to the pharmacy for a muscle relaxant. I think I need to stop going to parties with limbo contests!

I realized that I needed some wholesome exercise to de-stress, and

what better way is there to do that than to do some flying and boating? So I took the mountain flight over the eastern Himalayan range with a close-up view of Mount Everest, also known as Sagarmatha, sitting at a height of 29,000 feet. The Himalayas (Sanskrit for 'abode of snow') reveal to us visitors the incredible natural beauty of the landscape and the gorgeous unforgettable faces of people originating from Central Asia, Tibet, and India. The soaring peaks and plunging valleys isolate the populous so much that a herder-farmer in one family may speak a different language than his neighbors in the next valley.

After landing, we took a white-water rafting trip down the Trisuli River with our guides, Prem Sahi and Sete Lama. Navigating the fury of the high rapids, we got drenched! I thought we were going to flip over twice. I shivered a bit but 'got over the rapids.' Along the way, we saw many village folks and so many incredible birds: white breasted kingfisher, black drangol, sandpiper, white-capped river chap, and whistling thrush. As we continued our rafting, we held on with one hand and put the other in the air, acting like we were bull-riding.

Whatever floats your boat!

We ended our wild journey at Double Decker Beach and set up camp with our tents. Believe it or not, I volunteered to make the latrine! Remembering my Camp Blue Star days, I dug a huge hole located back a bit from our campsite. I tied logs together to make a square seat. I didn't do a half-ass job! It worked great. I was named the Latrine Queen. What an honor!

Prem and Sete cooked us dinner made of Skush, a green plant-like pear, and buffalo-buttered bread. Then we 'put another log on the fire' for chai. It was a glorious night spent in the tranquility of rushing waterfalls and a full moon under the great canopy of twinkling stars. Oooooommmmm!!!

The next morning, we plunged through the gorges of the Himalayan rivers, traveling through rocks and canyons in rugged white-water rapids, passing villages of different tribes, friendly and curious with darling children. We all dove into the icy river and swam with the rapids alongside the raft. Great exercise. (Better than going to the gym!)

After rafting, we stopped for a visit with a Nepalese guru at Ali Baba's ashram. He wore only a loincloth and had only one arm, as he had cut his other one off for a sacrifice to the gods.

We took a bus into town to Mugling, singing along the way, where we saw primitive natives with lots of jewelry in their noses. There were tribes of beautiful women with burgundy velvet dresses and scarf-like hats, all gold studded with jewels.

After making another attempt to reach Susan, I finally got through two hours later. Using the phone was such a big production. You're forever waiting, spelling names, and repeating numbers.

Linda and I hitched a ride on a tractor with a surprised old man to the Fewa Guest House. Linda didn't like bike riding, so I set out alone with pockets full of rupees, riding through villages, back alleys, beautiful fields, and gorgeous scenery, including amazing villagers carrying loads of grasses, firewood, and supplies on their backs. I passed by an outrageously beautiful girl, all loaded down with straw, and had thoughts of taking her back to the U.S. and introducing her to *Vogue* magazine as a top model. I gave her my snake ring that I was wearing. All of the kids yelled out "Namaste," a respectful greeting, as I rode through.

I entered a Tibetan refugee camp that was created for the people who had escaped Tibet from China's control. After meeting one family, I agreed to sponsor a woman's little girl and send $15 a month to enable her to go to school. Her name was Tseten Wongmo, and she was six years old. Only her father, Khamgar, could speak English. He took me to the waterfall where, as a Sherpa, he takes other trekkers. I was also asked to sponsor another daughter, Dolma Tsering. I decided to send money to Dharamsala School for her, as well. As a souvenir, Dolma gave me a yak wool belt/camera holder. When I returned home, I was faithful in sending money for many years. I received many thank you letters and pictures from them.

I rode my bike back through the villages in pitch-black darkness, no lights, ringing my bell, dodging cows, pigs, and villagers. It was exciting and dangerous at the same time. I could feel my heart pumping as I continued my cycling into the unknown. Holy cow! Did I really do that? (It is so hard to believe what one can do when you're young!) I finally arrived at Phewa Restaurant and Rest House where old ladies were selling magic mushrooms and hash to the hippies.

CHAPTER 4

*"To travel is to discover that everyone is
wrong about other countries."*
Aldous Huxley

India – Kashmir

Namaste!

I exchanged $100 for 1400 rupees, (RS 1400), on the black market
and flew to Varanasi. Linda and I found a guide named Dipak to take
us to the Ganges River where we watched countless people carrying
baskets of sand on their heads while making their way up to a waiting
truck. The sand would be used in cement. What a picture! The little
kids begged, *"Bakshish! Bakshish!"* asking for tips or a cut of the action.
Dipak pointed out the temple where their head honcho, like a pope,
makes all the decisions.

We canoed past *ghats*, the steps leading down to the river. The most
famous ghat is called Dasaswarmeth. There were many people bathing,
washing clothes, brushing their teeth, praying in lotus position, Rasa
yoga, meditating, and exercising, all in the same body of water. This is
Hinduism's most religious place where, for thousands of years, pilgrims
have cleansed themselves of their sins and sought release from the cycle
of rebirth.

Varanasi is the oldest living city in the world, dating from the seventh
century B.C. The Ganges River starts its long course in the Himalayas

and continues through India. Every devout Hindu's ambition is to visit Varanasi at least once in their lifetime and, if possible, to die or be cremated there. We saw corpses wrapped in silk or linen on bamboo stretchers waiting their turn to be cremated on ghats. We saw men chanting and praying, wearing *langotas* (long loincloths).

Approximately 80 narrow streets lead up from the ghats to the city. Sidestepping holy cows, we wound our way through narrow streets to see the Shiva Golden Temple. Dipak drove us to Viswanatha Golden Temple, Monkey Durga Temple, and Sarnath where Buddha preached his first sermon.

Arriving at the big-boobed maiden statue of the deity Tara, Linda told me that was her new nickname for me. So I nicknamed her Tina, which is the Hindi word for 'girl.' That's how we became the dynamic duo, Tara and Tina. We saw drawings of the Bodhi tree, showing how it grew from the Bo tree in Sri Lanka under which Buddha was enlightened and found ultimate nirvana. Excavations by the British in 1836 now show ruins and old relics of lions, which were later adopted with similar images as the state emblem.

This region is known as the oriental super Switzerland and is full of valleys with gardens encircled by mountains. Kashmir survived the fall of the Moguls and became a holiday resort during the final decades of British rule in India. Here in the capital, Srinagar, considered the Venice of the East, we met Valentino, owner of our deluxe houseboat on the Dal Lake. This type of houseboat is referred to as a *shikara* and was constructed at the close of the last century due to the maharajah's edict prohibiting ownership of land by the Europeans.

Our floating home had three bedrooms, a dining and a living room, a veranda, and a sun deck. We stopped for a 'spot of chai' and naan and they smoked coconut-flavored shisha tobacco from a hookah; there were no drugs to smoke, only fruit-flavored tobacco. This is a custom in many countries in this region, usually enjoyed at teatime or after meals. *{.It reminded me of a purple caterpillar, sitting on a mushroom, I once knew in a past life.}* A guide named Valentino joined us and we took our shikara back across the lake to the Shalimar Gardens. Nothing quite equals being pulled across the sky's reflection, bursting through lily pads and lotus flowers to the Shalimar Gardens—mountains, kingfish, and tulips, poetically proclaim Kashmir's lavish beauty.

Well, as far as I was concerned, it was time to shop until we dropped! We bought raw silk from Varanasi and gave it to a tailor to make jackets. I had a black dress made for $6 (60 rupees) from the raw silk I had purchased previously. At the wood-crafting shop, I designed my own 'lazy susan,' a rotating tray that holds several dishes for serving food. Mine would have an image of the goddess Parvati in the middle of it, holding bowls in each of her six hands. I paid 500 rupees, or about $50. I also ordered a walnut desk and four tables that fit inside each other with carvings of Hindu gods and goddesses: Ganesh, Parvati, Durga, Lakshmi, Brama, Shiva, and Krishna. I arranged for it to be delivered to the port of the United States.

Travel Tip: Although the products in Kashmir are considered the crème de la crème, one has to watch out for the merchants with a hungry mentality trying to rip you off a bit. Be warned! Buyer beware!

At 5:30 a.m., I woke up to Islamic chanting to Allah. I was freezing my *ashram* off. The hot water bottles that we had to sleep with in order to keep warm at night had lost their heat, of course. Br-r-r! Under their shawls, the Muslims wear a sort of portable central heating: a small wicker basket with a metal pan in which the glowing coals of charcoal, or *kangri*, are stored.

Hashish is in high demand in some neighboring countries. Valentino's uncle showed us how he smuggles hash, in compressed resin form, to other countries, using a painting, a framed picture or books. One picture of the Goddesses Lakshmi and Parvati had $90 worth of hash inside. I wondered if I should send one to my musician friend Willie N. in the States?

As the morning moved into day, the air was so hot and sunny that I was able to strip away my turtleneck sweater and put on a bathing suit. At the gardens, everyone was staring at the Westerners exposing their skin—a freedom not accepted by their customs. I found it funny to watch their eyes and surprised expressions. As we traveled in the houseboat, we passed by villages where we watched people scrubbing their clothes on rocks, beating them on poles, and even jumping up and down on them to get them clean. The mountain people, known as Shaferds, camp right in the middle of the rice fields. They travel from sunny Jammu to Sonamarg in winter and then return in the summer, caring for their animals.

After we departed the boat, we visited a carpet factory and watched how they made silk carpets by hand. I had them make one for me. I asked the designer to add two birds: a kingfisher and bulbul, the native Kashmiri bird. I also had Hindu writing added on the border and my name in Arabic on top. It cost me $600. They tie each tiny knot separately, so it often takes six months to a year to make just one carpet, depending on the size and intricacy.

It had been absolutely delicious to lie on our pillows, and bask in the sun throughout the day, but sunset started to fall upon us. Br-r-r-r-r, chatter-chatter! We rushed like lightning to get back into our warmer layers of clothes. Back at the boat, Valentino greeted us with Jungle Juice, local wine, and dinner. He made several passes at me, as usual, and said he wanted to meet me under the mango tree but not to eat mangos. He was a real Don Juan. I declined his offer for a moonlit shikara ride and went to bed with my hot water bottle instead.

CHAPTER 5

"The gladdest moment in human life,
me thinks, is a departure into unknown lands."
Sir Richard Burton

India – Agra, Jaipur, Udaipur

I had to say goodbye to Linda because she had run out of vacation time. A first class train ticket on the Taj Express took me to Agra. From there, a rickshaw took me to the Oberoi for a massage, manicure, and pedicure. Three people were working on me all at the same time, and it only cost me $7. Pure heaven.

Wow! The Taj Mahal was actually as stunning as I had heard it to be. It is the aesthetic epitome of a civilization. Shah Jahan had it built as a monument of love to his wife, Nur Jahary, who married him in 1612. She became *Mumtazul-Zamani*, bearing him 14 kids. Tragically, she died giving childbirth in 1630 at Burhanpeer where her husband was waging a battle campaign. When she died, the Shah put away his royal robes for simple white Muslim clothes and had the extravagant memorial built by 20,000 laborers. He brought skilled craftsmen from Persia, Turkey, France, Italy, and of course India to accomplish the incredible feat.

The huge mass of white marble resting on red sandstone is a jewel, fashioned over 17 years, with verses of the entire Quran reproduced on its walls. The inlaid designs contain jasper, agate, lapis lazuli, cornelian,

and bloodstone. One flower, for example, contains 60 different inlays only one inch square! Under the dome lies not only the tomb of his wife but also of Shah Jahan, himself; his son built it to bring the two of them to rest in eternity together.

I made two new friends at the Taj Mahal who took me to see the Fatehpur Sikri, the ghost capital of Akbar the Great, a complex of ruins from forts, palaces, and mosques. We went to the marble factory where they showed how raw emeralds, rubies, and other stones are cut, polished, designed, and inlaid into marble resembling the Taj.

They are put into tables, lamps, boxes, and figurines. I ordered a fabulous table.

Later in the day, I rented a cheap hotel for only $3. I met two Polish girls there and we agreed to wake early to go to a bird sanctuary at 4:30 a.m. It was a breeding ground for birds coming from as far away as Siberia. Our early morning nature walk was fantastic, seeing birds, doves, herons, purple coots, parrots, and dabchicks. We caught a local bus to Jaipur, which was a little crammed, but not impossible. We stopped twice for local weird foods and snacks for which I don't even have names!

The two girls talked me into saying I was Polish in order to receive a discount on hotels and rickshaws. Of course, if local merchants, hotels, and transportation workers heard you were from the U.S.A., they'd jack up the price. If you say you're Polish, they cut it in half. My line was "Me no speak English. Me from Poland." They bought it. Finally, we took a rickshaw tour of the city, stopping at Prostitute Street where we paid 30 rupees, (RS 30), or about $3, for singing, dancing, and an instrumental performance.

I loved Jaipur. The people were the friendliest I had met, but it was a little weird: there were camels, cows, and buffaloes walking down the streets and carrying heavy loads, and most everyone was working hard, especially at night. Poor people lived in communal tents with food carts everywhere. I met six Israeli people in the room next door and I stayed up all night, talking to them. They told me they lived in a kibbutz in Israel and had been traveling for eight months.

For 45 rupees (about $1.20 apiece), a sweet man with a striking gaze in his jet black eyes, became our rickshaw driver and tour guide for us three Polish tourists. We went to the City Palace where a maharajah still lived. A blend of traditional Rajasthani and Mughal art and architecture, the City Palace housed the hall of public audience, decor of intricate designs, and tons of marble everywhere. There were remarkable museums of carpets from Pakistan, beautiful hand-painted story pictures dating from the 17th century, and amazing Sanskrit writings from the ancient Hindu bible.

We went to the pink Amber Palace, the ancient capital of Jaipur, and the Rajput Palace on a hillside overlooking the lake where elephants typically escort visitors up the hill. The Palace included unbelievable gardens and a small temple with a statue of Goddess Kali, my favorite gruesome goddess (she had several heads, tongue sticking out, and garland of skulls placed around her neck). She symbolized the reincarnation of Parvati, the consort of Lord Shiva. The whole thing was built of marble with teeny tiny little mirrors on the walls and ceilings, making this mirror-style design very typical of Rajasthan.

We visited a textile factory where I personally designed and bought a Rajasthani-patterned skirt and vest. It was made out of old-fashioned squares of hand embroidery with tiny mirrors stitched in. These craftsmen have been famous for centuries for stone-cutting, enameling, setting precious stones, tie-dying textiles, block printing silks, ivory carving, lacquering, and brass-wear work. The tailor put it together right in front of me. Then he took my long black skirt and made a continuous pocket all the way around the hem to hide my passport and money. However, I have to admit that no one tried to steal from me. Instead, people ran after me to return my purse when I absentmindedly left it somewhere!

Our driver took us to the famous movie, *Sharaabi*, a love story about a rich man, played by the handsome Amitab Buchan. In the movie, the man falls in love with a dancer from a lower caste, which forbade them to marry. Although we didn't understand the dialogue in Hindi, the drama, thrills, crying, laughing, dancing, singing, bloodshed, and fighting kept us on track with the storyline. During intermission, I asked a man seated nearby to confirm that we understood the movie correctly. He didn't speak English very well either, but he and his friends tried to explain the plot. Around these parts, you don't ever talk to just one local; there will always be a group surrounding the conversation, curious to hear what the foreigner has to say. The people in India were so kind, warm, gentle, and helpful. I loved them!

Udaipur

I woke up at 4:00 a.m. full of energy and ready to fly to Udaipur. Gee, I thought, I'm going to have to stop working so hard trying to see everything and go everywhere! I need a vacation!

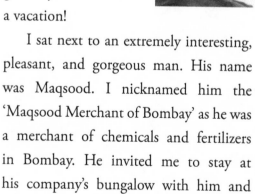

I sat next to an extremely interesting, pleasant, and gorgeous man. His name was Maqsood. I nicknamed him the 'Maqsood Merchant of Bombay' as he was a merchant of chemicals and fertilizers in Bombay. He invited me to stay at his company's bungalow with him and his friends. It was an absolute mansion.

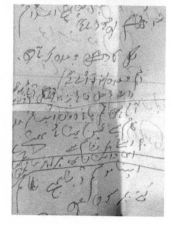

We went to dinner at Hotel Lakend for vegetable patty cutlets, milk rose, and fried *paneer* (cheese). We toured the fairytale city of lakes, fountains, and birds, The Abode of Kings, palaces, forts, and gardens.

Maqsood played music like a rock star, including one of the songs from the *Sharaabi* movie, and I wanted to learn it. I had a brainstorm! I noticed that one can write in Hindi very fast like we learned in shorthand in school, so I suggested that he write it in Hindi and then translate it for me in words that I could pronounce. It worked! He made the cassette for me on my recorder. In return, I gave him my cassette of Michael Jackson's *Thriller*. Such a deal! We each felt we got the better bargain.

We all sat around relaxing and talking for hours. Maqsood held one of my hands, and, not wanting to feel left out, Sharma held the other. They were darling. I really enjoyed their warm company and friendship. Maqsood spoke of love, telling me he loved me more than salt. He explained that you have to have salt on your food or else it's no good. To my amazement, there were no hassles about sleeping arrangements (after I said I had a headache.) We all slept peacefully in one king-sized bed. It was very sweet: a ménage à trois without sex. *Salaam Alaikum.*

CHAPTER 6

"When overseas you learn more about your own country,
than you do the place you're visiting."
Clint Borgen

India – Goa

My flight to Goa took me to Calangute Beach Hotel in the market area. The sixty-two miles of Goa coastline are endowed with some of the loveliest beaches in the world. It sort of reminded me of Mount Lavina Beach in Sri Lanka. Tucked between the ghats and the Arabian Sea, Goa blends scenic beauty with a Latin heritage and a leisurely way of life: palm trees, mango groves, and jackfruit trees interspersed with paddy fields, slumbering villages, temples, and shrines. The Goan people speak a different language, called *Konkani. Deo-boram-koru.* (Thank you.) I arrived in the midst of their annual New Year festival, the Diwali Festival of Lights, when people throw rice and toss sweets in honor of goddess Lakshmi and consort Vishnu. I met three nice chaps from Bombay. They were Pankaj, Dass, and Devender, and we became good friends. We all went to the Taj Hotel, which was magnificent with buffet dining and dancing. After the band stopped playing, everyone went to the beach for more music, drum beating, fireworks, and the burning of the villains of the goddess of prosperity.

Devender was a doctor, and he and I took a bus to Colva Beach. The bus broke down so we had to catch another one. The second bus couldn't cross the broken bridge, so we got onto a third bus. Finally, after two hours of trying to get to the darn beach, we arrived, but it was so bloody filthy, we couldn't stand the smell. Little white worms that looked like leeches were crawling around us....Aha! This was a fishing beach. No wonder people come here only to see the fishermen.

Arriving back at the hotel, we met Enrique, a chiropractor from Cuba, who was kind enough to give me an adjustment. I had wanted one since my back muscles had tightened in Kashmir from the stress of finding so many shopping bargains! The two guys, plus Tony, the local stud, went to swim in the beach. Tony sang on my recorder in the Goan language of Konkani. He said he was the Official Sex Instructor. First lesson free! Then he demonstrated karate for me on my movie camera. I got a ride back to the hotel on some kid's bike handlebars while I sang him my Hindi song.

I rode motorcycles with the Bombay boys to Vagator, a nude beach with young non-conformists from other countries, living worthlessly in shacks by a pretty fresh water spring but just *hanging out. (Get it?)* After Pankaj and his friends left, I went back to Calangute Beach to watch the sunset. There were so many people there, living in grass huts. They were dressed fashionably in saris and flashy jewelry, a status symbol, even in poor villages.

I found myself alone for the first time after seven weeks, watching a magnificent sunset. It looked like a ball of fire reflected on the sea: huge surfing waves, low clouds on one side, blue sky on the other. Birds were flying overhead, and the sky around the sun was turning a bright pink and red. I was in a meditative state, enjoying the sounds of silence. While I was loving my state of calm, a young kid carrying a canister of massage oils walked up to me and offered a massage. I said in a determined tone, "Chloe, chloe." Which means to go away. He did.

The place was really a hangout with Goans, foreign tourists, and hippies from all over the world *escaping* their lives at home. Everyone blended together. I met two new friends from Iran: Petru and Jalal, and his Aussie friend and champion kickboxer, Mad Mick from Jindivik. He thought he was really cool. They lived in a 'pigpoo-house' where the pigs slide through a tunnel and scramble to eat last night's leftover dinner.

Tony showed up and we went to Hotel Bain de Sol in Baga, jumping over the fence for the last time to get to my hotel instead of walking through the door. (I had to do this in dedication to my mom who told me to stop jumping over fireplugs and fences when I was a teenager.)

When I arrived at Indian Airlines to depart Goa, I was faced with an issue at the customer service desk. Apparently, there was an expiration date on my ticket, and consequently, the representative told me that my ticket had no value. I took matters into my own hands and left the airport. I noticed the ticket was written in red ink, so I used my secret weapon, my own red pen, to alter the expiration date on my ticket. I decided to stay an extra night to avoid having to interact with the same employee.

The next morning, I woke up and headed straight to the airport to go to Mysore. I put on my best poker face, and luckily, there was another representative on duty, and she accepted my ticket. Was I supposed to throw the ticket away and just put my hard-earned money in the trash? I don't think so! I can play that game, too!

CHAPTER 7

"The use of travel is to regulate imagination
by reality, and instead of thinking how things
may be, to see them as they are."
Samuel Johnson

India – Mysore, Ooty

It was the 31st of October. Halloween. I felt like something weird might happen today. Will it be a trick or a treat? I took a rickshaw to a sandalwood shop. I was in the middle of the store, holding a goddess sculptured from sandalwood, when an announcement came on the radio. Everyone became deathly silent. "INDIRA GANDHI SHOT DEAD" said the announcer. Two of the prime minister's security guards had murdered her at 11:00 a.m. at her residence. The first assassin opened fire with a .38 service revolver as she walked from her house to her office. The second opened up with his Sten submachine gun. Ironically enough, they shot her 16 times, the same number as the years that she served as India's prime minister. The Indo-Tibetan border police on duty at the guardhouse surrounded the assassins and shot them immediately. They later identified the assassins as sub-inspector Beant Singh, 33, and Constable Satwant Singh, 21. It was an inside job.

All of the shops, restaurants, and businesses shut down immediately. There was a tremendous amount of commotion, and very shortly after,

INDIRA SHOT

Assassination to be probed

NEW DELHI, Nov. 1
Prime Minister Rajiv Gan

Two security turn assassins

N

PRIME Minister Indira Ga
noon a few hours after her
her with a sten gun and a pisto

More than a dozen doctors, includ
surgeons, made frantic attempts to save
in vain.

According to hospital sources, Mrs. Gandh

Mourners from five continents

NEW DELHI, Nov 3 (PTI)
A total of the delegations from
five continents and international organisations were

pay their last respects to
Gandhi.
Fifty-one countries
wedded by leaders

Mr. Rajiv Gandhi, who
flew back to Delhi, cutting
short his West Bengal tour,
arrived at the institute shortly after 2 p.m.

Mrs. Gandhi was walking from
her residence at No. 1 Safdarjung
Road to the adjoining House No.
1 Akbar Road when two security
guards shot at her from their sten
guns. According to eyewitnesses,
as Mrs. Gandhi fell down there
was a shriek from members of the
household, including Mrs. Sonia
Gandhi, who rushed to the scene.
Other security men shot down
the two assailants.

Matador driver Umer Singh was
not seriously injured.

All roads leading to Mrs Gandhi's residence at No.1 Safdarjang
road were cordoned off immediately and the police and
security measures reinforced.
Steel helmeted and gun toting
cops were seen all over the place.
Huge crowds had gathered at

the AIIMS.
institute were
One of the
involved in th
identified as
The consta
police was
powered.

All the
rushed to the

Rajiv new P

NEW DELHI, Oct. 31 (PTI)   Shortly be

DEAD

vendors handed out newspapers like hotcakes. Rioting and total chaos
in the streets ensued and everyone threw stones at shops that had not
closed. Mobs were knocked down with vicious bloody fighting that
broke out. Yikes! This was the scariest Halloween I had ever experienced!

I rushed back to my hotel and jumped into bed. I literally trembled
with fear but was also saddened for these poor Indian people. Indira,
considered the most powerful woman in the world, had guided these
people for 15 years, and, like Mahatma Gandhi, she met with a tragic
end. After being around some of the sweetest people I've ever met, I
couldn't help sharing in their deeply-felt sorrow. I felt so depressed for
them. I felt like they had lost their mother.

Due to the death of Prime Minister Indira Gandhi, I could not
continue my journey to Ooty. Mourners stopped our tour bus halfway
on the way to the little town. Hundreds of people were marching with
black flags and blocking the roads preventing transportation and they

told us we should either be home in mourning or join in the walking parade of rioters. We all had to get off the bus. As I sat on the grass in the shade, not knowing what the hell to do, nine curious little girls surrounded me. Trying to remain calm, I persuaded them to sing the Indian National Anthem into my cassette tape recorder as we waited, not really knowing what was going to happen next.

The newspapers reported stories of mobs on the rampage all over the country. They were burning cars, buses, and rickshaws, and the crowds attacked each other in many communities, especially Sikhs, who bore the blame for the assassination. Roads were blocked, and security was tight near the borders, especially in Pakistan. Violence erupted, with bombs bursting in the air. Many people had set up Indira's pictures, framed with flowers, incense, and burning oil lamps in little enclosures to pay their respects and to grieve. According to the newspapers, the nation plunged into widespread grief and the entire world felt it. Officials swore in Rajiv, Indira's son, as the new prime minister.

Our bus driver decided to try to sneak the bus, with us inside, through the roadblocks, using excuses like taking medicine to his dying mother. We passed by deer and peacocks along the wildlife sanctuary, a beautiful dam with a waterfall, and a huge blue lake. The bus began to overheat, and I sacrificed my water bag to cool off the engine. That got us only a few kilometers. We needed more water. I suggested we gather water from the lake nearby to pour on the engine, but the driver didn't take my advice. Huh? *Why not?*

There was no hope for this bus ride, so we grabbed our belongings and jumped onto another bus heading to Ooty. I sat next to a man who had some fruit and nuts with him and he kindly offered some to me. I was so hungry! After all these years of my mother telling me to clean my plate because 'people are starving in India,' this was such a turnabout. Now, the Indian was feeding the starving American!

The bus was disassembled at the next stop, and everyone seemed to scatter. So, there I was, left alone, not only grieving for Indira Gandhi's death but also for my own misfortune.

I sat all alone on a hill watching the sun go down and wondered how to get out of my predicament. All of a sudden, three tiny boys, about eight years old, appeared before me on three horses, and offered me a ride. I thought I was hallucinating. Two of the boys each took a backpack and the third boy took me! We rode off into the sunset! I couldn't help but have a realization: when you're in the depths of depression, in a real 'twilight zone,' someone is always there to help you. This is the true India!

The boys took me to Hotel Raja in Ooty. Once I settled in, I went to the local market to find some food, and it was there I came to meet Sini. He turned out to be one of the nicest guys I met on my entire trip. He took me to his home to get some milk, and then we made another stop at a friend's house where we gathered more food supplies and a friend of his. The three of us continued to the next friend's house to gather more food and then we were four.

We made a few more stops to pick up other ingredients, and we stayed at a house with a fondue pot. We all made a wonderful dinner of lentils, dahl, chiku and ramphel fruits, samosas, masala dosa, and saag paneer. Other friends dropped in, and finally, there were ten of us. It would have been alarming otherwise, but since I had been here for some time and understood the culture, I was very comfortable. We discussed politics, the election of Reagan, Gandhi's policies, and the U.S. practice of giving aid to Pakistan and not India.

Continuing my journey by train, I had to push my way to a first class compartment, which cost 35 RS. Second class was 8 RS, but it was so crowded, people were hanging off the side of the train. They were on top of each other. We had to make stops at Mettupalayam and Coimbatore. I had to sit in my compartment for three hours on the way to Cochin. Several curious locals accompanied me, wanting to speak English with the American girl traveling alone.

The group got off at the next stop. Just when I thought I might get some peace, eight very tall African men from the Nigerian Navy entered to share the compartment with me. I felt very intimidated and small, especially when they seemed to be getting comfortable to spend the night. *{So I reached in my pocket for a piece of the cookie I had been saving and popped it in my mouth and got bigger. It was the one in the package that said, 'Eat Me'}* Finally, the conductor sent them out and a family of three locals—a husband, wife, and little girl—took their place. Thank Lord Shiva for getting me out of that one!

Once the family got situated, they immediately switched off the light and went to sleep. I had to make my bed in the dark. I brushed my teeth, spitting out the train window, because I was afraid of leaving my compartment with all my belongings there. This was India; nothing could surprise me anymore.

After 14 years of constantly traveling, I had never known anything like this country. I had to hang in there and survive. I wondered what would be my next shock? The funny thing about it was that I have been amused at every bit of this drama! I always wore Indian clothes and wore the red round *tika* on my forehead. This country made me feel at home. *Namaste.*

CHAPTER 8

*"Every man can transform the world
from one of monotony and drabness to one of
excitement and adventure."*
Irving Wallace

India – Cochin, Kerala Province

It was around 6:00 a.m. when the rickshaw guy, Vijay, took me from the railway station to the ferry across Ernakulam Lake. The trip required taking another rickshaw and hopping onto a rowboat across Vallarpadam Lake to Bolgatty Palace Hotel. I chose the place because it was far away from the riots due to the assassination. After an hour of doing my wash in a bucket like the locals, I went to the hotel pool to take a swim. It looked filthy, but it was cleaner than the Ganges. My dad only told me not to swim in the Ganges. I ended the night watching Gandhi's cremation service on TV with a few locals.

One of my contacts, named Chitra, invited me to stay with her and her three teen-aged children. She took me for a tour to see the Chinese fishing nets and their oldest synagogue, Paradesi. It was built in 1568 and was covered in old scrolls and tiles from Canton, China. Jewish people were supposed to have fled here when Nebuchadnezzar occupied Jerusalem in 587 B.C. (Note: The oldest synagogue in the world is in Prague.)

I started wondering if my parents were worried about me, as

newspapers were filled with stories of wild riots and killings over Indira's murder. Over 1,000 people had been killed so far. People were committing suicide, being beaten to death, and being burned alive. Some resorted to shaving their heads and parading around in gloom and grief. Curfews had been imposed in 30 cities, and 50,000 Sikhs were missing, either dead or hiding out in refugee camps from the Hindu mobs. The turmoil had set in.

I heard that the news programs in the U.S. were reporting that American tourists were being persecuted and killed because the Soviet Press blamed the assassination on America. They were claiming that the Central Intelligence Agency was responsible for the slaying. I decided to call home to let my parents know I was okay. It was the perfect decision, as they were absolutely sick from worry and thought that this time was the ultimate and they had really lost me. I assured everyone that I was staying with a nice, comfortable family and they shouldn't worry. In fact, I was introduced to Chitra by one of our Indian stewards on the airplane. She had a luxurious home with statues all over the house and even a fountain in the foyer.

Chitra's son and husband, Lok and Lakshmi, took me to see the famous Kathakali dancing, well known for ancient religious pantomime dances from the epics of Ramayana, Mahabharata, and Puranas. The techniques go back 2000 years. Colorful costumes and outrageous eye movements interpret stories of love and demons.

Kerala Province

After flying to Trivandrum, I arrived at Kovalam Beach at the Orion Lodge close to the ocean to hear the waves in my ears as I slept. The cutest 13-year-old boy, Krishna, checked me in. I rushed out to jump into the biggest waves I'd seen in my whole life. The current was strong. Krishna warned me not to go out too far and told me that four guys had drowned last week. But I decided to push the boundaries. (There I go again!) I watched my step, I mean my stroke. It was incredible. Waves 20 feet high rushed toward me on both sides. I swam and fought the sudsy waves all through the sunset. I even stayed in the water to watch the sky turn pink and the moon appear in full. It was magical. I adore being at the beach.

Touring, trekking, temples, and traveling may be tremendous, but having been a mermaid in a past life, my relationship with wonderful warm water with wicked waves on a tropical paradise island is my weakness. It's my nirvana!

I rose at dawn in the land of magic surf, Kerala, a palm-fringed paradise in the tropics. It was one of India's most remote regions. Kerala is a thin strip on the southwest coast facing the Arabian Sea. The tale of its creation goes something like this: Parasurama, an incarnation of Lord Vishnu, after slaying 21 kings, threw his battle axe into the sea. From shaft to blade, the land of Kerala sprang up in its place.

On this beautiful beach, women wore saris of many beautiful colors. Saris are the typical Indian long dresses. They are worn differently in each area of the country to blend with the culture and climate. In the North, some are dressy and wrap over the shoulder; in the South, women wrap the cloth around the waist (lungi-style); on the beaches, there are variations between the two. One will find more silk in the north where there are larger cities of wealthier castes.

Coconut oil is used for everything! I bought freshly squeezed coconut oil, and a man appeared and asked for some. He rubbed it on his face and all over his head, giving his dried afro the Michael Jackson look.

My experience of purchasing goods had matured greatly by this point. I finally realized how much a coconut (or anything else) really sold for, and I didn't have to ask and haggle over the price. I learned to silently give the salesman three rupees (25¢), and he would know that I knew the right price and he could not jack it up to this American. I used my new knowledge to buy banana chips and crackers to carry with me because I was never certain when I would get my next meal. I knew from experience not to take that chance again. It made me realize how a human being can feel when they are starving. That empty feeling I had in my gut while enduring the bus ride was overwhelming. Have you ever had that feeling? It is a feeling of panic. It made me sad to think about how many starving people in the world suffer with that same feeling every day.

I woke up sick and weak with 'Delhi Belly.' What did I eat or drink wrong? Everyone was trying to make me feel better. Krishna brought me ginger tea, and one of the schoolgirls insisted I eat a red banana, drink salt water, and circle my head three times with a rupee. I went back to bed, with Krishna sleeping on his mat near my door. He said he was my bodyguard now.

Chapter 9

"Man cannot discover new oceans unless
he has the courage to lose sight of the shore."
Andre Gide

Maldives

As I was on the southern tip of India, I decided to seize the moment
and take advantage of where I was. I flew to the Maldive Islands and
took a speedboat to the island of Feruna. The beaches of Feruna feature
beautiful shades of blue water and golden sand. The shallowness of
the water reminded me of Hikkaduwa in Ceylon. The Maldives
Archipelago is a group of over
1000 tiny coral atolls, whose
southern tip lies on the equator
basking in the blue Indian
Ocean. Feruna's government is
an independent republic, and
the island has approximately
150,000 people. Dhivehi, the

Maldivian language, is similar to Sinhala used in Sri Lanka. They
export black coral jewelry, mother-of-pearl, and tortoise shells.

I finally did my first scuba dive there. It was so incredible and made
me remember why I worked so hard for the last seven months to make
an extra $8,000 for my trip. We went 90 feet deep for 50 minutes.

It was my ocean form of meditation. It was an incredible wonderland of tranquility. The coral and fish were beautiful, abundant, friendly, and close enough that we could pet them. We actually fed sharks right out of our hands. Some of the sharks were six feet long, and one swam within three inches of my face. We explored reef walls, finding several five-foot-long grey moray eels opening and closing their mouth showing sharp teeth. Tons of other fish were there, especially white zebra fish and parrotfish. My dive master, Mani, on our night dive, carried the torch, and we went down 30 feet for 30 minutes. Can you imagine diving at night... in the dark?

I saw crab, square blowfish, colorful deadly poisonous scorpion fish, barracudas, doctor fish, and needle fish. The most gorgeous sight was from shining the torch through the jellyfish. In the day-light, jellyfish just look white and trans-lucent, but at night, you can see tiny pink colors going down their vein on one side

and tiny bluish-green colors coming up their vein on the other. I never saw anything like it before. Unbelievable! I felt sorry for people who are afraid of the water and scuba diving. They are missing some of the most incredible sights in the world. The last starfish I saw was bigger than a beach ball in circumference.

A new load of people arrived overnight. My favorite: the Aussies. I heard their familiar way of speaking the 'Queen's English' as they 'raged' all night in the lounge. I met three of them chatting in front of the bungalow. One of them gave me his Australian T-shirt. It said,

See Alice while she's Hot, referring to Alice Springs in Ayers Rocks, of course. It had a picture of the rock on top. I gave him a Maldives T-shirt for a swap.

I sunned on the beach, and rearranged my schedule *again*. I had to continually re-plan my next move because I always seemed to end up wanting to stay where I was. Later that night, I watched a movie with Mani, listened to my German tape, and danced backwards.

On one dive with the whole group, we dove with manta rays in Manta Reef and found one huge stingray about five feet in diameter with an extended barbed-stinger tail. Our last dive was to be through very narrow caves. *{I felt like I needed to be smaller, so I drank from the little glass bottle with the tag, Drink Me.}*

After the Aussies left, Mani walked me to the boat pier. He gave me a going away present—a kawaii shell, like the one he wore around his neck. We took a speedboat to the airport where I met another traveler. We sat together and compared our experiences. She had traveled for six months already and had come down with a cold, the flu, typhoid, and malaria and, thankfully, recovered from all four. She had completely different experiences than I had had.

I arrived back in Kovalam Beach where all of my friends from all over the world were still hanging out. I gave my little bodyguard, Krishna, a T-shirt with a shark on it.

I had finally returned to coconuts for lunch and crashing waves in Kovalam Beach with my previous group of traveling friends. I ate breakfast next door with the locals. We had hot, spicy salad and chapati, served on a large metal plate called a *thali*. The dipping sauces were in little bowls called *katories*.

I met a kind, loving couple from Bethlehem, S.L. and Joy Anne, and we had an interesting conversation that included their disappointment that Reagan had won the U.S. presidential election. They said if he kept up his ridiculous policies, other countries were going to start closing their doors to America's travelers, India being one of the first. Everyone I met on this side of the ocean was also disappointed with Reagan and thought he was a joke, especially for interfering with Nicaragua's troubles and giving aid to Pakistan. S.L. and Joy Anne and I have remained close over the years.

After a fantastic dinner consisting of lobster and champagne with a few local friends, I tore myself away from the beach to continue my journey. Krishna's brother, Ganesh, carried my bags through the jungle, and I flew to Madras. By the time I arrived, I had chills and a fever, so I stayed in the New Victoria Hotel, a more decent and expensive hotel than I would usually pick. I didn't know what the hell was wrong with me. I didn't know what illness I had, so I didn't know what to take to relieve my pains.

Chapter 10

"Stop worrying about the potholes in the road
and enjoy the journey."
Babs Hoffman

India – Madras

The morning newspapers told of a cyclone devastating the area in Hyderabad, which was not far away, and a hurricane battering Madras, where I found myself. Army, Navy, and Air Force were called for relief. I hoped no one at home would worry about my well-being.

Originally, I had planned to explore Madras, but I felt so weak and feverish that I lacked the energy to get out of bed. Jain, the hotel houseboy, came by to check on me. He brought sweet *lassi*, a yogurt drink, to settle my stomach. I began to think how devastating it would be if I ended up with some awful disease. I gave in and finally decided to see a doctor, as all of the hotel staff has been urging me to do so.

The man from the travel agency downstairs put me in a rickshaw because I was too weak to walk even a short block. I was taken to see Dr. Rajan on 14 Kennet Lane. He recorded a fever of 101 degrees. He diagnosed me with viral pneumonitis with gastritis and pharyngitis. He gave me two injections: one of Baralga and the other Betnesol. The total cost for the checkup and prescriptions was 50 RS total, less than $5.

I took a rickshaw back to the hotel and sweated out my fever while reading *Tales of Krishna*. I eventually crashed and got some time to recharge my batteries. I woke up feeling rejuvenated. I guess I got sick because it is such hard work (and play) traveling in India. Even the guidebooks warn you to take periodic rests while traveling in this country! Even the sun can be scorching and can cause dehydration. I'd started to look like Mahatma Gandhi when he went on his hunger strike.

Since I felt better, I decided to get on the road again. I went to the post office to get newly issued Indira Gandhi stamps.

CHAPTER 11

"A mind that is stretched by a new experience
can never go back to its old dimensions."
Oliver Wendell Holmes

India – Pondicherry

I hopped on a bus to go to the ashram in Pondicherry, hoping to find my inner peace, as the Beatles had done there. While riding the bus, I read a book about Jassa Singh Ahlu to get an idea about Sikhs. I arrived way past sunset and did not know where to go. Santosh, a lady who was staying at the guesthouse near Sri Aurobindo Ashram rescued me when she asked if I'd like to come with her. It's a good thing I met her because I had no idea that I wouldn't be able to get a place to stay so late at night. I would have been stuck in the middle of nowhere in the dark. We asked the head guru, an older man dressed in white, and he gave me a room. I noticed everyone was dressed in white. It looked to me as if everyone was floating around instead of walking. 'Where the hell am I?' I thought.

My eyes popped open at 5:00 a.m. and I was full of energy, anxious to see the ashram, a world commune of love. It was founded by philosopher, poet, and patriot, Sri Aurobindo. He was exiled there in 1910 after political strife. His ideal goal was to be a superman who surpassed his fellow man in the things of the spirit. I could hear religious chanting beyond the darkness of not quite dawn.

At 6:30 a.m., I had tea with Santash, and we went to the communal dining hall for breakfast. There was an assembly line for food and then everyone sat around on the floor. We were given flowers and incense to place on the center table and all bowed down to give honor to Sri Aurobindo. All of the religious followers sat around humming, bowing, and praying. It was kinda bizarre. They led us to the bed where their blessed Mother had died 15 years ago. Here, we all knelt and meditated.

We left to go to a few little shops to buy silk, books, batik, and souvenirs. But I wasn't there to shop; I was there to find my inner peace. They told me to go back to my room to relax and do nothing, absolutely nothing, but meditate all day. I had allowed three days on my schedule for that, but I decided that I wasn't going to find inner calm that fast, so I changed my mind and left.

I took a taxi, dodging water buffaloes that were carrying huge loads and led by men with whips. I arrived at Serenity Beach, which was filled with free-spirited youths just hanging out. Again? This was very unappealing so I hopped on a bus back to Madras. I never knew that this country was a hippie haven. Hippies were everywhere!

I arrived in Madras all alone in the dark, with my bags in tow, surrounded by dark strangers. (Indians in the north are a lot lighter skinned.) No one spoke English, and there wasn't a taxi in sight. I took a big gulp, grabbed my bags nervously, and found a tri-rickshaw, a cart attached to a bicycle and driven by an older man. The funny part of being in tri-rickshaws is traveling up a hill. You have to get off and help push. And you're paying for it!

At the hotel, the ceiling fan wasn't working. (It was always *something*, but usually it was the toilet!) The hotel porter came to fix it, and that led to a very interesting conversation. He was well educated and wanted to talk to the nice lady from United States. Everyone seemed to think that all Americans were wealthy, while they felt stuck in poverty. I told him

I worked very hard for money to travel there. He said that he wanted to work very hard, also, but there was not enough employment for everyone. So, what could they do? We discussed their overpopulation problem and lack of decent opportunities. It made me really appreciate what I had and reminded me to be thankful.

I realized that the next day was Thanksgiving. While everyone was home eating turkey, cranberries, corn, and stuffing, I would be drinking *lassi*, a yogurt-based drink, which would be good for my upset stomach.

I ordered a lassi from room service, as I felt a bit weak from the trials and tribulations of the day before. After I finished bathing and drying myself, I noticed the towels looked gray from all of the dirt and dust. I shuddered to think of what was coming that night since I was planning to go to Calcutta, which is considered the armpit of the nation. It was the only way to get to Burma, and there was only a night flight. Yikes! But I felt I had to keep moving because staying in place could mean falling behind!

India was a weirdly interesting country, filled with paradoxes. On the one hand, there were countless palaces. They were clean, beautiful, and absolutely stunning and refreshing. On the other hand, I needed to mentally prepare myself for going to Calcutta, which, as the guidebook had warned me, was 'a place like a cancer, eating at the flesh of a nation, covered knee deep in the fallout of India's population explosion.'

India had the best and worst of everything, and you could get almost anything you needed. It would take you two hours to get an airline ticket confirmed but two minutes to get a watch fixed.

CHAPTER 12

"All journeys have secret destinations
of which the traveler is unaware."
Martin Buber

India – Calcutta (Sick with a Sikh)

I woke up feeling sick, like there was a knot in my throat, and my
stomach pains were at it again. Could it be something serious after all,
like my liver? I was so weak and felt helpless. However, I managed to
get to the airport for my flight to Calcutta.

*Newsflash: A local Bombay train derailed, killing many people. No
solution to slum problem in Madras after severe cyclone lashed the city last
week and slum dwellers waded through water to their huts.*

There was always something horrific happening in their country.
India is so unpredictable. I hoped I would get out okay.

I took the airport bus to Oberoi Grand. The traffic there was the
worst I had seen in the entire world. I called a contact from Tamir, a
passenger I had met on a flight almost a year ago, and he agreed to meet
me at my hotel. It shocked me a little when a guy wearing a turban
walked into my room. After all, I had become very leery of Sikhs by
then, due to the death of Gandhi.

The contact's name was Jali Bhandari, and he turned out to be a
very honorable guy. He took me to his parents' house, where he lived.
We visited for a long time. His mother was a sweetheart and sang

and played accordion into my tape recorder for me. Jali's father and I discussed the Sikh situation, Punjab, wars and troubles, and separation of East and West Pakistan.

Jali was a big tennis pro and traveled all around the world, staying with families and playing tennis. He was the second top player in Calcutta, and rated third in India. He removed his turban for me because I was curious, and all of his long, black, silky hair came tumbling down. It's against their religion to cut their hair or shave their face.

Jali's cook made a gourmet meal of at least 20 dishes of fabulous-looking foods, but my stomach started doing flips, and I couldn't even touch it. Could I take it all to go, please?

Learning of my gastrointestinal discomforts, they called the family doctor who took a look at all of my prescribed medications. He told me to throw them all away except for Vitamin B syrup. Then he prescribed two other medicines: an antacid, and another medicine to increase the level of my blood pressure. *What?* Every doctor has told me different things and giving me different medicines.

'Where's my dad? He's the doctor I need!' I thought.

The next morning, Jali and his parents took me to Hotel Hindustan to see a wedding take place. The time-consuming rituals they went through were unbelievable. The bride and groom sat on throne-like chairs and dipped their hands in a number of concoctions while the priest read from the *Shruti*, the Hindu bible. After a couple of hours, they walked around a small fire several times. They sat back down with bowls of spices and flowers. A huge buffet of hot, spicy foods followed. Everyone enjoyed time to mingle and visit other guests. Both bride and groom were well dressed; she had a nose ring chained to her ear. Very flashy! All the guests wore elaborate saris and suits. The ceremony lasted seven hours.

I woke up at 3:00 a.m., itching all over, with my stomach on fire. I felt like I needed nourishment so I ordered ice cream and cake. I figured I'd go out in style. I called Susan, who was taking care of my schedule, and told her that she should know I might have hepatitis, in case I didn't make it home. But every time I suggested that I thought I had it, the doctors would say, "Nahi" (No), no problem, and that I would be okay.

It might have been my imagination, but I thought the whites of my eyes were looking yellow with jaundice. I had all the right symptoms. I couldn't understand why I'd been to three doctors, been prescribed tons of medication, and after telling them it might be hepatitis, they all laughed! I wished I could kick the heels of my ruby red slippers and be home, but that was Dorothy, not Alice. I was so exhausted, it was hard to continue writing in my journal, but I had to force myself with every ounce of strength I could muster. There I was, on the complete opposite side of the world from home, lingering on the threshold of death.

I thought, 'I've got a long way to go but a short time to get there. Someone, unlock this door and get me out of here. H-E-L-P!'

I finally took it upon myself to figure things out! I took a single-man-running rickshaw into the burly, sweaty giant of traffic jams, penniless peasants, bearded Sikhs, sari'd Hindus, holy Muslims, and sacred cows of almost ten million people to the Belle Vue Clinic. The large population was due to the partition of India and Pakistan in 1947 when Hindus, by the millions, flooded into India, fleeing their homes. The problem was later repeated in the Pakistan/Bangladesh war of 1972.

The intern behind the counter said I should give him a urine specimen because it was a lot cheaper ($5) than a blood test. I opted for the blood test because I wasn't in the mood to die in Calcutta over a $25 blood exam. When the lab report came back, it showed a severe case of hepatitis, with liver-function counts way off the charts! I had been right all along! Oh my goodness! Why didn't I get this information from the doctors?

After that, I had the most fun-filled, action-packed day of my vacation: I did not leave my hotel bed except to go to the bathroom! Jali brought me liver pills and glucose. Later, his friend Chanda brought me fresh vegetable soup, Vitamin B syrup, two coconuts, and sugarcane juice. He wanted to put rosewood sticks on my forehead for 24 hours as a magic cure-all. They brought me a TV, which didn't work, but I was too tired and weak to keep my eyes open anyway.

I finally had enough energy to take my first bath in three days. All the parts of my body that weren't tanned from the sun were pale yellow. My parents called and were very alarmed over their 'Yellow Paige.'

I had stomach cramps and pains all day, and I could not eat the papaya that I had ordered, so the houseboy cut it for me and fed me. I could not help myself.

Travel Tips:
Lesson #1: Don't get hepatitis.
Lesson #2: If you do, don't let them put beans in your vegetable plate or you'll be playing the trumpet.

So, there I was, with excruciating pains but with journal in hand, recording the whole horror story! I felt like a turbojet ready to take off any minute.

♫ The pain that's mean comes mainly from the beans.
I think I've got it...I know I've got it! ♫

A visitor from the hotel brought me flowers, and a lady from the U.S. Embassy came to check up on the Sick American. She had me admitted into the Belle Vue (Catholic) Clinic. Praise the Lord! I could finally get some uninteresting, bland food that wouldn't give me gas pains.

To my horror, the first meal was tomatoes, spicy rice, and lamb. According to the doctor's instructions, I wasn't supposed to eat anything acidic, anything with meat, or anything spicy! I may as well have been eating pizzas and Big Macs. Next came banana pudding, but I wasn't supposed to eat anything with creamy sauce. Insane! Immediate gas pains began again. Sister Daphne gave me some Pepto-Bismol.

Teatime brought a houseboy with hot tea, even though I was supposed to drink cool beverages only. He started trying to raise my bed straight up, even though I was supposed to lie flat to keep my liver in a horizontal position. What kind of place was this? If I had listened to all of the doctors and hadn't taken the initiative to get my own blood test, what would have become of me?

Two of the nurses had been mixing my coconut water with gaseous mineral water. *Are you joking?* They tried to be neat, but they were actually messing everything up. They kept trying to put my things away and put my coconuts in the closet. I had to keep getting up out of bed to get them out of the closet or else I'd forget about them and they'd all rot. Two young sisters walked in as I was taking the coconuts out of the closet and started giggling and ran out. They caught me twice. I had to laugh, too, but it was about time I laughed after all my misery and 'liver quivers.' Chanda came by and put a circle of rosewood sticks on my head. It's an ancient custom of healing. It's supposed to grow down to my shoulders in three hours. It had already been eight hours, and nothing was growing! Nice try!

CHAPTER 13

"One's destination is never a place,
but a new way of seeing things."
Henry Miller

India – Calcutta (Belle Vue Clinic)

A doctor finally arrived. Dr. Rupak Mitra, gastroenterologist, was the only doctor that seemed to know what he was doing. He asked all the right questions, used the right terms, and said that I needed to take as few medications as necessary. Finally!

As he examined me, he crossed out all of the prescriptions on the chart made by other doctors. He said that he would alternate visits with Dr. Varma. What's with this custom? Everyone does things in pairs. Two bellboys carry one bag each, instead of one guy taking both small bags.

The houseboys share towel responsibility: one hands you the towel and the other gives you a washcloth. It goes on and on, but I didn't expect it from doctors. It is probably because there is a shortage of employment. Everyone wants a piece of the action.

Dr. Mitra left, saying he'd be back the next day. Then, as Dr. Varma was about to leave, he said he'd see me the day after. So, I informed him that I didn't think it was necessary for both of them to come. He admitted I was right since Dr. Varma was actually an eyes, ears, nose, and throat doctor. HUH?? Five doctors later, maybe Dr. Mitra will save me. They have so many gods and goddesses to pray to, who do I pick? I need *all* of them.

I woke up at 3:00 a.m. with my stomach on fire. (Again.) Help! I rang my bed bell to call for antacid medicine but fell back asleep. At 6:30, my door burst open, and two nurses rushed in and yanked open the curtains. The sun blinded my yellowy eyes with light as they sat me in a chair to change my bed sheets. I was trying to protest that the sheets didn't need changing because I was not supposed to wake up early. The main objective of my getting well was to rest and sleep. After they left, I snuck the two sheets that they had removed from my bed and stuffed them in a pillowcase for a better pillow. Finally, maybe I could sleep better. I closed the curtains and went back to bed.

At 8:30 a.m., a male nurse came barging into the room with a

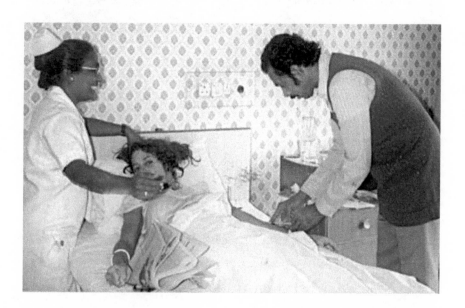

syringe to take a blood test. I told him, "Stop! You've got the wrong patient. I just had that done yesterday. It won't have changed yet. I heard Dr. Mitra say I needed to get a blood test in four days! Not now!" The nurse grabbed my arm anyway, forced it down, tied the rubber around it, and drew out heaps of blood. Then, he grabbed my other hand and pricked my finger for another bit of blood.

An hour later, a nurse came in with a thermometer and offered me coffee. Doesn't anyone read my chart? I am not supposed to have any of this happening, but I am supposed to have breakfast. This is all I get? Coffee? Not even juice?

Finally, Dr. Mitra walked in, and I felt like Superman had finally arrived. I told him what had happened and he couldn't believe it. He was furious at them because I was right! I worried that if the nurses didn't follow his instructions, they might end up taking my appendix! On top of all the drama, men were working on the roof, sawing and hammering, making it very hard to sleep and to get well.

Lesson #3: Don't ever get sick in a foreign land, especially Calcutta. Dr. Mitra told me there are ten million people and only two specialists in gastrointestinal illness.

The nurses had a schedule shift and brought me very bland food of boiled fish, carrots, bland rice, and raw papaya. They served papaya to me every day, as it is a natural healer and contains papain, an enzyme that digests proteins. It contains potassium, magnesium, many vitamins, and antioxidant nutrients, which promote heart health and protect against colon cancer. I should write an article on 101 ways to prepare papaya.

By that time, my body had become so weak and lifeless; they had to hold me up to pour coconut juice down my throat. I had another nurse take a picture of them surrounding my yellow body. I also drank coconut juice every day as it is also a natural healer. It is rich in nutrients, reduces blood pressure, promotes hydration, and is also helpful in curing headaches and hangovers. I'll toast to that!

Another aide came in to take my blood. I almost jumped out the window. Sister Daphne assured me it was Dr. Mitra's orders this time. They were draining me dry!

♫ How dry I am... too weak for rovin'.
As they steal all... my hemoglobin. ♫

My goodness, what a bunch of vampires! Thirsty for American borscht! Why don't they just *beet* it.

I talked to my Mom and Dad on the phone. They were worried sick that I might die there. As Bob Dylan would say...

♫ Hey Mama, could this really be the end?
To be stuck inside Calcutta with the Mobile blues again. ♫

After breakfast, I exploded like a bomb. I was so weak. I took my first shower since I arrived in Belle Vue and only because the nurses kept insisting on it. I felt so frail standing up that long that I absolutely collapsed before I could get back to the bed.

Superman Mitra came to check out my 'liver quiver' and to talk about an incubation period. Could I have picked up this vile illness from food, water, *what*?

Meanwhile, the shower had zapped all my energy. I couldn't hold my head up, and the nurse had to feed me lying on my side. Lunch consisted of rice and dahl with a yellowish sauce. All I could do was lie around all day and be handfed. What a relaxing vacation! Barf.

At 5:00 p.m., I looked at the clock and realized I had not had one gas pain all day. Yea, it's like Christmas! Or Hanukkah! Did it Passover? It's like a day of atonement without the tones. (And it's five o'clock somewhere, so I need a drink! Just kidding.)

I tried to sleep as much as I could, but the nurses kept waking me up to give me more vitamins. Are you *kidding*? Darn it. They pulled me out of a deep sleep for that? I didn't think it was necessary when I could have been doing all that at mealtimes. If it weren't the damnedest place! I had to beg for clean towels and toilet paper.

I started to figure that maybe I'd bargain with them the next time. I'd cooperate with blood tests if they would give me the supplies I needed. Maybe I'd raid the linen closet if someone would carry me there. I figured I could ask the patient next door who was only half paralyzed. Sister Daas told me to take my medicine, and I told her, "Not until I get toilet paper."

Dr. Mitra came by again. He smiled and laughed a lot (especially when he read my daily journal), and put me in a good mood. I felt like I was getting healed from the sickness because his fun personality made me come out of my depths of depression to laugh with him, even though it hurt to laugh. Laughter was my best healing drug!

The next morning I woke up to find myself still alive. Woohoo!

The night before, I had been in absolute pain for three hours and kept crawling back and forth to the bathroom. AGONY! It was so torturous that I popped a sleeping pill, not caring that it might destroy a chunk of what's left of my liver. Flirting with the chance that I might not wake up again, I wrote a few goodbye notes because I was too weak to write a will.

It made me stop and think. I thought about the special people in my life: Fannie, our family nanny who stole my heart from our first encounter when I was 13 years old. I reflected on my family, friends, and, of course, my favorite cowboys. A big tear rolled down my cheek as I recalled so many poignant experiences. Even cowgirls get the blues.

I remember thinking, 'I cannot believe that this is my fate: to be stuck in a health clinic in Calcutta, India, dying, while my family was on the other side of the world!' I realized that when my body was helpless, my mind was the only thing I had left to keep me going, so I started to compensate for it by putting my brain on overload. I found that it made my writings funnier, and I was helping to *heal with humor*, too. I couldn't help but start to reminisce about all the things that had led up to that moment......

Originally, I had planned to study nursing in college. I wanted to try to keep the tradition of medicine in my family running strong, so I took physics and chemistry classes. "Stop!" said my #1 cousin, Beth. She convinced me to change my mind with her perspective that 'college years aren't supposed to be that stressful, but rather a time to party and enjoy yourself.' So, I rerouted my course away from medicine, realizing that maybe I should focus on the skills at which I was a natural wiz. I majored in English grammar and literature and began student teaching.

Eric was the most troublesome little second grader I encountered as a student teacher. One day, when he was being really naughty, I teased him, "If you keep misbehaving, I'm going to karate chop you!" (I had taken karate lessons since high school.) But the little tyrant took a right swing and punched me right in my solar plexus! On that day in 1969 I decided to give up *swings* and go for my *wings*. From that moment on, I knew I did not want to teach about the world, I wanted to see it for myself!

It's unbelievable to look back and think how this one miniscule incident transformed my entire perspective and put me on the journey of wanderlust!

As I looked back on all I accomplished and the experiences I captured, I realized that little seven-year-old Eric, who had caused me to find a career that satisfied my desire to travel, deserved my heartfelt gratitude.

Thanks to computers, google and advantages of modern-day technology, I recently decided to reach out to Eric. I simply found his picture and info in the proper photo album of my college days. I called him and told him that because of him, I had been traveling all over the world. I learned that he had become a mechanic, married, and has three kids. He had never left Tuscaloosa, Alabama. I told him my story and I thanked him. In his most southern twang, he said, "I sure am glad I could oblige ya."

So lying in a clinic bed in Calcutta, I started thinking about the amusing life I had lived before this trip. . When I graduated from stewardess school, I was young and full of curiosity. My greatest ambition was to get myself to Hawaii, where I imagined myself in grass skirts with coconut shells over my mammary glands. It became my goal to get there on my first vacation as a sky goddess!

CHAPTER 14

"Remember that happiness is a way of travel –
not a destination."
Roy M. Goodman

Flashbacks: Hawaii

Aloha!

What a freakin' paradise! My roommates, Joy and Mimi, and I were surrounded by soft Hawaiian music and peaceful easy feelings everywhere. I recommend this amazing place for a honeymoon. The first tasks were to take hula lessons, surf, and learn how to make crafts with coconuts and frond leaves. We were enticed to visit the *Don Ho Show*. We loved his fun-filled act and bubbling personality, especially when he sang, "Tiny Bubbles." After the show, we were picked among several other ladies to attend a backstage meeting of the Hawaiian superstar.

The highlight was when he invited me to be his date to the after-hours entertainment party in someone's mansion. It was the most incredible party I have ever attended. In every room, there was something different going on; Get-down-get-funky dancing was in the largest area. Other rooms included an enormous food buffet, several gambling tables, group-singing with a piano player, and a huge bar with soft music. In the last room, there was a gigantic indoor adult pool party. It was an amazing night for me, an innocent 22-year-old

at the time, but Don Ho was a perfect gentleman and made me feel cmfortable. I was so impressed with this cool dude that I studied and learned his signature song, 'Tiny Bubbles' in the Hawaiian language.

CHAPTER 15

"To travel is to live."
Hans Christian Andersen

Scandinavia

My next trip took me to Norway and Denmark with a couple of friends. After a snow-filled skiing trip in Voss, we continued to Copenhagen, the home of Hans Christian Andersen's Little Mermaid, a small bronze statue by Edvard Eriksen that is displayed on a rock by the waterside. It looked similar to Walt Disney's mermaid, Ariel!

Scandinavia was also famous for other things: one being pornography. This trip took place at a time so many years ago that Americans then couldn't fathom that they could actually see a magazine with nude people in it, not even in *Playboy* magazine. We really were not interested except we felt like we wanted to take advantage of our situation. We decided to go to a porno movie, just so we could check it off our list of things to do before we die. One friend, Sharon K., was a devout Christian and very shy. She didn't feel comfortable going to the movie but she didn't want to be left alone either. After the movie, I asked her what she thought of it and she said, "I never opened my eyes."

Years later, I decided to *finish* my Scandinavian journey in a *Finnish* way by going to Finland, as well as to Sweden. I went to the Laplands in Finland to see Santa Claus and the reindeer farm at the North Pole. I actually did that on a long layover from Helsinki with a quickie detour to Estonia.

Sweden is the last of the Big Four countries in Scandinavia, so the following week, I chilled out in the Ice Bar in Sweden on a long Stockholm layover. Everything was made out of ice, even the drinking glasses. The bar, tables, sofa, and chairs have been chiseled from ice blocks. Fortunately, we were given a thick, goose-down, padded, long jacket upon entering so I didn't freeze my *tuchus* off!

CHAPTER 16

"Not all those who wander are lost."
J.R.R. Tolkien

Afghanistan

My memories of Afghanistan started in 1979 with my move to Marina Del Rey, California. I shared an apartment with my old college (RollTide) hell-raisin' hillbilly friend, Norman, from sweet home Alabama. This Willie Nelson fan founded the famous J. BUCKS SHIRT COMPANY and entertained with magic tricks on the side. Next door to us was our neighbor, Hakim, who was from Kabul. We became instant friends, as I had always been curious about his country.

He noticed my passion for international travel and discovery and finally said to me, "Hey, would you like to visit and stay with my family in Kabul? My room is available since I am here."

Well, guess what? He didn't have to ask twice!

I quickly became a part of the family once I arrived. The house was full of family because it is the custom when one marries to bring their spouse home to their parents and live all together. Since we had a full house, every meal was a party. Woohoo! A huge plastic tablecloth was spread on the floor, and we sat on the floor and ate with our hands, using our thumbs to scoop the food into our mouths, even the rice and gravy. We had damp cloth rags to help us stay clean, fortunately. My favorite dish was *subzi paneer* (baked cheese with spinach).

Our most interesting excursion with the family was in Bamyan Province to the Afghan Grand Canyon, 230 square miles of soaring cliffs and cascading lakes on the edge of the Hindukush Mountains.

We talked and laughed a lot, discussing the differences in our customs. I even wore a *burqa*, an Islamic garment that covers the whole body with a net screening covering the eyes. They laughed at this silly foreigner when I snuck up on one of the family members with, "Hello, it's me!" Women wear burqas so they cannot be seen...duh.

Everyone I met was so kind and friendly. I learned some of the language. What sounded like 'Ka-tima da sch-tor sh-war mi-shi' meant 'Would you like to ride a camel with me?' Of course, they taught me two songs, the second one about Allah. I wore a little wooden cross to show I was Christian, so they wouldn't know I was Jewish. (Mom was worried when I told her the head of the household was named Mohammed.)

I told Mohammed that I wanted to wake up at 5:00 a.m. to kneel on the prayer rug and pray with them and kinda get into the culture. When he came to wake me up, he didn't just tap me on the shoulder, he actually tried to get into bed with me! I yelped and jumped out of the bed!

The incident was never addressed for the remainder of my stay. I'm sure there was a miscommunication on his part, as it is not hard to do when coming from different cultural backgrounds. Their women are so restricted and they associate American women with free love. But I never did ask him to wake me up again! He turned out to be a sweet, harmless old man, and I grew to love this wonderful family!

In fact, I loved them all so much and had such an amazing time that I wanted to stay an extra week. While I was trying to find the nerve to call in sick at work when I was actually healthy, I saw some girls eating strawberry ice cream. When I told them I wanted one, they said that my American stomach couldn't handle the un-pasteurized milk and that I would be sick and vomiting for seveal hours. Sick? That was the perfect opportunity I needed. I bought two strawberry cones, and, sure enough, I was throwing up my guts within an hour. It was lovely. What a girl will do for love!

I called my supervisor and told him about my condition. He said, "You are where? Are you kidding me? Hang up quick! This is really a long distance, expensive call. I'll take care of it." I was overjoyed because I was able to stay an extra week with the family I had grown so close with. They played keyboards and bongos and we all sang together and had a real blast!

The day after I left this delightful family, (December 24, 1979), this wonderful country was blasted by the Russians! (I was so sad for them, but I was so glad for myself that I did not eat more ice cream.) Years later, I found out that the family escaped and was safe, living in California.

Islands

I spent a good amount of time swimming, sailing, surfing, sunning, snorkeling, and scuba diving in Aruba, Belize, Bermuda, Bimini, Guadeloupe, Puerto Rico, Greek islands, Caymans, St. Barts, St. Maarten, St. John, St. Thomas, Dominica, Key Largo, Fire Island, Corsica, Guam, Palau, Guadeloupe, Turks and Caicos, and Saipan. They all seemed to have a few things in common: music, dancing, happiness, no worries, stay on island time (it's five o'clock somewhere), flip-flops, beach life, and freedom from stress. It is magic to wake up every morning wondering what new flower, plant, bird, fish, sunrise or sunset I would discover!

In Spain's Mallorca and Menorca, I joined my old friend Hans from Holland. These islands, with their sun-bleached shores, turquoise waters, and rocky coastlines, are long-time playgrounds of Europe's elite. We stayed with his famous gay artist friends where we had luxurious parties every night with billionaires from around the world.

CHAPTER 17

"Traveling – it leaves you speechless,
then turns you into a storyteller."
Ibn Battuta

Ecuador (Galapagos, Amazon Jungle)

Buenos dias!

Once I caught my breath and decided to start traveling again, my best friend Sherry talked me into going to Quito, Ecuador. First, we visited the equatorial monument, the Mitad del Mundo, (middle of the world) at 0° latitude! Our next stop was an outdoor vegetable market with the largest and most beautiful fruits and vegetables imaginable. However, as we were walking through the crowd, a man with a dagger slashed my silk handbag in half and grabbed all my money, my camera, film, and traveler's checks. Luckily, I was able to grab the most valuable item, my passport, as I saw it tumbling to the ground. That afternoon, I spent many hours filling out paperwork at the American Embassy.

We were heading south and had heard of the therapeutic mineral mud baths at the bottom of volcanoes. We had stupidly hitched a ride from some guys in a jeep. We didn't think it was stupid at the time because we had done it as teenagers. I reckon we grew up with a hillbilly mentality that *everybody* was real darn hospitable in Mobile. (You know, down yonder there in Ala-damn-bama.) Anyway, we put our backpacks in their car, and the guys told us that we could stand on the back bumper and hold on; they wouldn't be going very fast.

However, they started speeding up, and I am sure they thought that they could have some fun with us and scare us. Or that we might let go and fall off the truck, and they could get our bags. Even though we were paralyzed with fear, we held on for dear life through the curvy, bumpy roads, our hearts pounding. We felt powerless but determined not to surrender our strength! We thought it was the end for us, but we made it. We spent the remainder of the day in the mud baths! Kumbaya!

Our next death-defying ride was with a man in another jeep as we continued to head south. We managed to get seats in the vehicle this time, but it had been raining so hard that the driver was worried about the descending slippery road. He stopped because it was too foggy, and he could barely see the winding road in front of him. We stopped to get out of the jeep and look and it was perfect timing. There was NO MORE ROAD! It had washed away, and we would have driven off the cliff if we hadn't stopped. After taking a deep breath, we turned back and headed up the road to safety. Hallelujah!

Sherry and I decided to take buses from then on. We traveled down the Andes Mountains and visited several indigenous villages. We hung out with the locals and enjoyed being in their markets, but would end up sleeping at bed and breakfast places every night. When we reached Guayaquil, we took a flight to the Galapagos Islands, where life has taken a course unhindered by man. The islands remain as living laboratories of evolution.

We boarded the ship *Sabella* and spent the next ten days discovering the most amazing reptiles, iguanas, tortoises, penguins, and mammals. We saw dolphins, lizards, batfish, manta rays, and scorpions. We went snorkeling with the sea lions, angelfish, and sharks in lava holes, and we went scuba diving with the fur seals. It was so entertaining to have them actually brush up against our tanks and engage us in a game. They would get in front of us and look back wondering why we were so slow.

We were surrounded by the most gorgeous birds: vermilion flycatcher, swallow-tailed gull, oystercatcher, Galapagos dove, yellow warbler, and the blue-footed booby.

The Galapagos are important to science because it was Darwin's visit there that started him on the train of thought that culminated in his book, *The Origin of the Species*, which then revolutionized our view of nature.

One of the highlights of the trip was interacting with the people on the ship. We became friends with everyone and it felt like one big family. When Valentine's Day arrived, we wrote poems to everyone. Our two favorite friends were Pat from Canada and Arnold from England. After years of keeping in contact, I found myself rowing along beautiful Lake

Louise with Pat's family in Alberta, Canada. Arnold was a jolly good ol' chap who took us yachting on his 32-footer, *The Rose of York*, in Southampton. He wore his British yellow *wellies*. His ambition was simply to cruise around the world in his yacht!

Although we were warned of the border conflict between Peru, Ecuador, and the western side of the Amazon, we continued our journey to the Amazon jungle. Most of the tribes we came across were not dangerous, but we were told to stay away from the Pygmies because of their savage rituals. For example, the chief witch doctor would kill a young villager, cut his head off, and throw the headless body to the hungry crocodiles. The Pygmies worshipped crocodiles, so that was a way of keeping them happy. They would then shrink the young man's head. To do so, the brain was removed,

and the empty skull was packed with red-hot sand. After 40 days of repeatedly replacing the sand, they'd boil the skull in a special brew for two weeks and then dry it in the sun for two more weeks. When they were finished, the skull would be the size of an orange. Gee, what a treasure to take home and hang from my ceiling. *(Would I do that?)* Sorry about the gore, but, unfortunately, this is their culture.

CHAPTER 18

"Two roads diverged in a wood and
I took the one less traveled by."
Robert Frost

Bahamas

On one of my earliest dive trips, I met
with some danger in the Bahamas. I was
on a typical dive boat, in the Atlantic
Ocean, and the captain reported that
the current was calm and he expected
it to be a beautiful day. I jumped off
the boat with the other divers, but I
must have been distracted; I didn't
realize my vest had been inflated and I
wasn't going down. I was confused and
flopped around like a fish out of water.
The people still on the boat started

yelling at me at the same time, so I could not figure out what anyone
was saying. My only real help came from the deaf girl. Why? She gave
me a gesture.

I dove down to about 70 feet. I had lost my designated swimming
'buddy' in the confusion, so I decided to bite the bullet and go by
myself. I was having an amazing time watching the fish and the

colorful kaleidoscope of corals when I looked down and saw that the kelp seemed to be drifting by very fast. I realized that we had run into a strong current and it was pulling me further and further out. I felt panic! Once I ascended to the surface, I could see the dive boat, but it looked like it was miles away. My heart was racing as I waved to them with my bright orange glove in distress.

After what seemed like an eternity, a lifeboat appeared to be coming to my rescue, but once it approached, it kept on going. My heart raced faster from the disappointment, and as I turned around, I saw the young, red-headed boy, Destyn, from my boat even further out than I was. He was in total anguish! The boat had gone to pick him up; I felt confused since it didn't seem to be returning for me. I started to feel very anxious, like they had not seen me, and then, I was frantic. I felt like Rose in *Titanic*, hanging onto a large piece of driftwood, crying out, "Come back! Come back!"

The lifeboat finally circled back to rescue me. After getting back on the dive boat, the young man and I sat in the boat with full composure as we made the return trip to the shore. It wasn't until after we had removed our gear and settled down that we started to drown in tears of relief of not drowning! (To this day, I cannot think about this story without crying.)

Kuwait

I had attended an airline holiday party at which I won a first class ticket for two on Kuwait Airways to go anywhere in the world. So my friend

Louise and I took off for the Kingdom of Kuwait. The only other people in the first class cabin were billionaire princes and sheiks in their long robes. Can you O.D. on caviar? We did! We met Hadi Mutairi, the pilot, and he and his friend turned out to be our guides the whole week we were there. We stayed at the Marriott, which was built like a ship. Years later we watched on

TV as that same hotel burned down in the Gulf War during Operation Desert Shield.

Of all things to happen in the world's richest country (according to the World Bank Atlas), the weirdest occurred to me. I cracked open a silver filling in my tooth. What bad luck to have to deal with a 'dark cloud' like this during my vacation. But Dr. Raja Liddawi, dental surgeon, replaced it with a 22ct. gold filling. For free! He said it was a pleasure to meet an American girl traveling in his country. *Really?* What a great souvenir! The expression, 'every cloud has a silver lining' surely was apropos for me. But I got a gold lining instead!

We went to a Bedouin Festival and learned about the craft of weaving Bedouin costumes and making jewelry, weapons, and food. We also entered a camel decoration competition. It was a riot, 'hamming up the humps!'

Sri Lanka

On to Sri Lanka. Louise and I took a quickie day tour to ride elephants and watch them bathing. We got so overheated that we just dove into the lake with them to cool off! The other people there were grabbing their cameras and going wild, saying, "Look at those crazy Americans." The young elephant handlers bathing the elephants were so shocked because elephants are one of the most deadly mammals in the world, and they could have easily turned on us for invading their territory. The elephant bathers were actually thrilled to have us in the water with them and admired our bravery. Looking back, this became one of my travel highlights! **It's also the story that influenced cousin Brad to motivate me to write a journal.**

Thus, the birth of this book!

CHAPTER 19

"Our happiest moments as tourists
always seem to come when we stumble upon one thing
while in pursuit of something else."
Lawrence Block

Australia

G'day, mate!

One of my most **take-your-breath-away** experiences occurred when we were scuba diving in the Great Barrier Reef of Australia. The beauty I witnessed was indescribable. Thirty species of whales, dolphins, and porpoises have been recorded on the reef, including the dwarf minke whale, Indo-Pacific dolphin, and the humpback whale.

There are also hundreds of species of brilliant multi-colored coral. But the most educational moment was discovering the Nudibranchs. In technical terms, the Nudibranch is a gastropod mollusk without a shell. It is basically a colorful snail. *Nudibranch* means 'naked gill,' and it refers to the feathery tentacles on its back. They are impressive but when touched, they can cause the human skin to blister or inflame. They usually travel in pairs, one on top of the other, and the Aussies refer to them as 'Nudis doing a naughty'!

Under water, the world's hidden gems were a constant unfolding of colors. At one point, I was so mesmerized that I broke the rules and wandered deeper than I was supposed to. I also lost my diving 'buddy.'

I felt infatuated in a magical trance of beauty. When I realized what had happened, I looked at my gauge—I was close to 120 feet deep, all alone!

'Yikes! What had I done?' I was getting good at this master-of-disaster drama. I was on the verge of a major panic, but I kept telling myself that I could deal with the situation. Nobody else could help me out of this one. I was stuck underwater, all alone, trying to be calm and not to hold my breath. I started ascending very slowly, careful to exhale methodically, stopping every ten feet for a few minutes until I finally reached safety.

I made it! Hallelujah! The Barrier Reef *literally* **almost took my breath away!**

I rested and ate Vegemite sandwiches. Vegemite is the staple for Australians. It is a black soft spread, something like our peanut butter, but made of vitamins, yeast, and vegetable extracts. It takes getting used to, however, I was there for almost three months, so, I got hooked! There are many ways to create your own delightful meal, but my favorite was to put the Vegemite on toasted bread, add cucumbers, alfalfa sprouts, and walnuts. Yummy!

There were other divers with their private yachts nearby, and we all met underwater! Once we surfaced, we got together and had 'bugs on the barbie.' (Bugs are a very common Australian crab-like fish found in the reef waters.) I joined the group instantly and found myself sailing with them for the next three weeks. There I was, in the middle of the Great Barrier Reef, on a private little sailboat, diving everywhere I wanted, with no rules or boundaries, with new 'blokes and sheilas'(boys and girls) who later became some of my best friends. What a spectacular feeling of fulfillment!

The biggest rock in the world, Ayers Rock, is in Alice Springs. I was eager to climb it at sunrise and then again at sunset to see the amazing differences and also to get a picture of me actually 'springing' in Alice Springs.

I now have a painting of Disney's Alice springing in front of Ayers Rock in my basement in the Australian room. All the rooms in my house are themed; each one is decorated like a different country. (Call for a tour!)

The majority of Australian aborigines lived in this area. When I saw them in the streets, I would sneak up behind them just to listen to them speak. Their speech patterns were captivating, something I had never heard before. There were a lot of guttural sounds and popping noises. *(Ta'nuk apaja'sitesk)* (How are you?)

When I visited the Wildlife Sanctuary, I heard someone right over my shoulders say "Hello, darling." I turned around and saw that it was a cockatoo. I was so impressed. Later, I heard about King's Cross,

a place famous for tattoos, even though I didn't know of anyone with a tattoo in 1981. I thought I'd get myself a tattoo of a cockatoo as a souvenir of my trip to the *Down Under*, giving me a magical memory of a favorite fascinating country. It was a souvenir never to be lost.

I became so enamored with the birds of Australia, I started getting up at 4 a.m. to see them. My favorite was the kookaburra as it sounded like human laughter.

Traveling to the opposite side of the country, I arrived at Perth, where I enjoyed the privilege of participating in sports history. I saw the world famous yacht race when Australia II beat America's Liberty and snatched the cup from America's grasp. *Good on ya, mates!* For 132 years, the prized trophy had made its home at the New York Yacht Club. This made Australia II the fastest 12-meter yacht in the world. Being with the Aussies for several months, feeling like I was one of them, even learning their language (Australiana), I felt obligated to participate in the celebrations with champagne and famous local Bundaberg rum! *No worries!*

CHAPTER 20

"People don't take trips, trips take people."
John Steinbeck

New Guinea

"Yu stap gut?"(How are you?)

Being on the other side of the world, I decided to follow my quest to go bungee-jumping in New Guinea. My new Aussie friend, Dundee, and I met and stayed with a couple in Mt. Hagen. To my horror, I noticed that they triple-locked and put chains on every door in the house. When I asked why, they told me that, at sundown, the young teenagers turned into hoodlums and loot, assault, and shoot their guns randomly.

The following day, Dundee and I were in the market in Port Moresby, taking in all of the activity, and lost track of time. When the sun finally started to go down, we remembered what we'd been told about the hoodlums and so we ran as fast as we could, with our purchases in native *bilum bags*, hanging down our backs, to get safely inside before sundown. Bilum bags are string bags made from sisal that the locals use to carry their market purchases. I found them to be very useful as they free up your hands (and backs). I loved them so much I still use them to this day.

There are 852 languages spoken in various parts of this country! I learned a bit of Pidgin English, the most widely used language in

New Guinea. It was amusing to converse with the local houseboy where I was staying.

The next morning, we walked through a valley to get to the Baiyer Bird Sanctuary and see the famous indigenous Birds of Paradise. The sight of the incredible creatures was an awesome and enriching experience. They are among the most fascinating on Earth and an extraordinary example of evolutionary adaptation.

All of a sudden, while we were observing the birds, it started to 'rain cats and dogs.' The water rose so high in the valley that we were unable to return. Oh my God, we were stuck! We prayed for a miracle!

Where was Moses when we needed him to part the waters and give us a path to walk through? Well, he did not appear; but, just as it was getting dark, half-naked natives with children showed up in a dugout canoe. The canoe had been made from a single tree trunk. Its once-rough bark felt smooth as silk from gliding through the water. They rescued us. We were so grateful to them for saving our lives that I gave them a little money, plastic airline wings and small toy airplanes for their kids, which I carried around to give away when traveling.

They took us to their jungle camp and treated us to a feast of taro, kaukau, rice, sago, pig, and yams. It was there that we met Father Tracy, a priest, who invited us to stay in his base camp, Yagusa Village Mission. To get there, we had to endure an unbelievable death-defying jeep drive over steep and slippery cliffs and through rivers. I still get chill bumps remembering the feeling of my heart in my throat! I do not know how, but we arrived safely at the mission house. We finally began to relax. But just as we started to step outside to take a walk, Father Tracy said, "By the way, don't go outside after dark. We are surrounded by cannibals."

Uh... Never mind!

New Zealand

I stayed with a couple in New Zealand who owned a dairy farm. They showed me how to milk a cow. I was handed a cup and was told to squirt the milk from the teet into the cup, as it is safe to drink it right away. So to be funny, I said, "Oh, no worries. I don't need a cup." They took photos of me squirting the milk straight into my mouth.

After hair-raising experiences in New Guinea, I loved my calm and relaxing time traveling in both the North and South islands of the land of the Maoris.

A few highlights of the trip included a cruise to a place called

Hole in the Rock, a drive through miles of green pastures of sheep and cows, birds, and waterfalls to the Glow Worm Cave and a magnificent flight in a ski plane over the Franz Josep Glacier. No danger there!

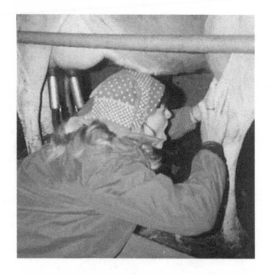

New Zealanders are called Kiwis (named after their Kiwi bird) are just as kind and hospitable as the Aussies. They're always laughing and they love to tell lots of jokes and keep you in good humor. The biggest difference between the two is that the Aussies have a more raging sense of humor and will say anything. So watch out!

CHAPTER 21

*"A traveler without observation
is a bird without wings."*
Moslih Eddin Saadi

Bali

I discovered the most beautiful sunsets in the whole world on Kuta Beach. Bali is one of the 17,500 islands in the Indonesian archipelago, known for its forested volcanic mountains, iconic rice paddies, beaches, and coral reefs on the Indian Ocean. It is also known for its yoga and meditation retreats. We were entertained at THE PUB by a little nine-

year-old kid who sang and danced for us. He had everyone laughing every evening with his off-the-wall jokes. He reminded me of Robin Williams. Note: Due to modern technology, I found him again, 30 years later through Google! (I have photos of when he was a little boy and after he became a man. Both pictures show him playing the guitar.)

In Ubud, Bali, I enjoyed delicious food, especially *rice tafel,* a combination plate of several Indonesian-Indian-type dishes. Ubud has one of the best museums of art I have ever seen. I was sneaking around taking pictures of some of the art when our guide saw me and told me that it was allowed. Wow, I was breaking a rule that wasn't even a rule.

> ***Travel Tip:*** Do not miss the Laksa coconut soup. (Actually,
> my favorite Laksa soup was found in Singapore where I
> went to the most beautiful Orchid Garden in Asia.)

At the monkey forest, we were told absolutely *not* to carry any food and not to pet the monkeys, even though they were adorable, because they could bite if they got annoyed. But there is always one traveler that just doesn't get it! In this case, she *got* it all right, as a monkey bit her, and she had to be rushed to the hospital for rabies shots. (No, it wasn't me!)

Tahiti

Ça va?!

On the way home, ending a four-month escapade in the *Down Under,* the plane made a stop in Tahiti, so I decided to jump off for one more experience. I couldn't help it. *The devil made me do it.* This South Pacific archipelago is shaped like a figure-8 with alluring black-sand beaches, water falls and volcanoes.

When I arrived, I saw a bike sitting up against a building and I thought it would be a unique and original thing to do to bike everywhere.

I explored each of the five islands by biking: Papeete, Moorea, Raiatea, Tahaa, and Bora Bora. Turns out James Michener had already said that the best way to see Bora Bora is from a bicycle seat. I can testify that he was correct. He also said that this island with its turquoise lagoon was the most beautiful place on earth. One must go there and see it to believe this enchantment.

CHAPTER 22

"You don't have to be rich to travel well."
Eugene Fodor

Jamaica

Wopnin' mon? (What's happening, man?)

I was so impressed with Jamaica: not only for its pristine beaches but for the daily gatherings at Rick's Cafe in Negril, which sat close to a challenging cliff from which people would dive. I was doubly impressed by the Rastafarians, for their cool outlook on life, their obsession with music, and their macho spirit. My dear friend Frank and I would sit and talk with them for hours.

Years later, I bought a pair of Bob Marley pants, T-shirt, and dreadlocks in a market in Tel Aviv. I wore them to a Halloween costume contest at our annual airline fundraiser luncheon and won the Best Costume prize. I wore the outfit again later, and sang with the Caribbean band, at a Caribbean dinner party!

♫ Don't you worry, bout a thing,
'cause every little thing's gonna be alright... ♫

The third time I was in Jamaica, I bought a Bob Marley doll. I put him in my suitcase but left his head sticking out of the top, just to be funny. As I lifted my bag up to put it on the belt to go through security, one of the security checkers saw it and said it was too cool. So, I started singing the words to Marley's song, *"Don't you worry 'bout a thing,"* and snappin' my fingers and strutting around. To my surprise, the eight security personnel joined me, and started doing the same thing. What a happening! They sang the whole song with me. Apparently, nobody cared about the cuticle scissors I had in my bag! They were just rockin' out.

    'Ya, mahn!'

Chapter 23

"A journey is best measured in friends, rather than miles."
Tim Cahill

U.S.A.

At the height of all of my exotic international travels, my brother Bruce asked me if I had even seen my own country. "What kind of a *Yankee Doodle* gal are you? Try some good ole' apple pie" he said. I was caught off guard! I knew he was right, and I decided to see every state in the U.S. before I went on another overseas adventure. I had already visited

about 30 states on layovers and snow-skiing trips, so why not make it another goal to conquer?

My old college friend, Willie T. (University of Miami) and I chose ten states to explore together on a road trip. With plenty of snacks and a lot of music, and after a majestically scenic skiing trip in Copper Springs, we started our road trip in Colorado.

After Colorado, we drove to the Grand Canyon, Painted Desert, Petrified Forest, Wyoming, Idaho and more. The most thrilling part of that trip was picking up petrified rocks in the Petrified Forest; their vibrant colors glistened in the sun so much they looked like jewels. The most difficult part of the trip was when I had to put the rocks back down due to the Park's regulation.

During a later ski trip to Sun Valley, Idaho, I remembered that one of my favorite celebrities owned a ski condo there. Never in my wildest dreams did I imagine that I would get the chance to ski with Clint Eastwood. It was kind of him to 'go ahead and make my day!'

Afterwards, I was overwhelmed when he asked me out for the evening, but I was too shy to accept. I suppose he wanted to 'go ahead and make my night'!

Skiing was always a fun-filled hoot with one of my favorite ski pals, Rae, another stewardess. She was always pulling tricks on me on the airplane and getting so out-of-control when she laughed that she would actually fall down. Her sense of humor and continuously happy laughter shined a ray of sunshine in every trip. You could say she brought the sunshine wherever she went, including the beach in Greece, where we got into a lot of mischief. But my lips are sealed on that one!

Continuing my quest to see more of America, I decided to go Country-Western style. Melinda, another Delta Stew and I decided to see more of our country through the rodeo circuit. We met real bull riders and they invited us to join them while they traveled around the country for competitions. She and I would attend a rodeo (and party, of course), then fly home to work a three-day trip to California, New York, or Vegas while the cowboys were driving to their next competition.

After a *glamorous* three days of serving 'coffee, tea or me,' we would fly to the next rodeo and unite with the same group once again. They traveled in trucks and trailers, hauling the bulls of the Wild West through the dirt and dust to places like Oklahoma, Ohio, Alabama, and Texas. Our favorites were Robert C. (his pet name was Diablo) and Rob McD., world champion bull riders. My heroes have always been cowboys. And that's no bull! It was a great way to see the U.S.A.: as cowgirls! *Yee-haw!*

Note: Through the years, due to Melinda's glamour and magnetism, I spent time with Pat Boone, Evil Knievel, Prince Faisel of Saudi Arabia, country music stars, and other exciting celebrities. However, the greatest, most fun-loving, amazing man she ever introduced me to was the talented Tom Lysiak, three-time All-Star center with the ice hockey team, Atlanta Flames, and later, the Chicago Blackhawks. In fact, she admired him so much that she simply took him off the market and married him!

These American trips were so refreshing that I decided to pick about ten more states and complete another road trip. I took my cousin this time and visited Yellowstone National Park, North Dakota, South Dakota, Mt. Rushmore, Nebraska, and more, thus completing 49 states. We even dressed like cowboys and Indians to take hilarious pictures throughout the trip with authentic backgrounds. It made us appreciate our land of liberty and spacious skies, from sea to shining sea!

Alaska

I continued towards my goal of reaching all 50 states by cruising through the glaciers of Alaska. However, the highlight of the trip was when we got to the Golden Heart City of Fairbanks, the jumping off point to the Arctic Circle. I jumped (actually flew) at the offer of the 75% airline discount, which was only available to airline personnel, on this very expensive flight to the top of the world, Point Barrow! I had to leave my cousin behind in a funky 'fear and loathing in Margaritaville' type of piano bar for the next few hours! But he was very understanding. He knew I was a culture-vulture and I wanted this rare opportunity to be with the authentic Eskimos in their own village.

When the small aircraft landed in Fairbanks, we were welcomed by smiling faces. It stays so frigid outside there that there's no need for refrigerators; they just dig a hole in the permafrost, a thick subsurface layer of soil that remains frozen, to store their food.

One young local Eskimo with two long thick braids flowing down his chest invited me to join him, along with his friends and family, for dinner and marijuana. (It was not medical but was very legal!) I hesitated, seriously thinking of what new and crazy experience it could be, but I was afraid of what I would be getting myself into next! I was very tempted!

Cowboy Cuzzin' Rodney

CHAPTER 24

"Once in a while it really hits people that
they don't have to experience the world
in the way they have been told to."
Alan Keightley

India – Calcutta (Still here?)

I was so excited with the temptation of a new experience, with an
eskimo, that it brought me back to the present time. I realized I was still
lying in a frigging hospital bed, and the only drugs I would encounter
were on my night table. There were seven bottles of medicines:

Aludrox - aluminum hydroxide gel - antacid
Polycrol Forte Gel - Antacid and laxative
Streptomagma - Anti-diarrhea
Calamine lotion for itching
Polybion Vitamin B
Liv. 52 - Liver tablets
Dilosyn – Anti-pruritic and anti-allergy

None of these medicines would cure me. They would only aid in
complications. The only way to heal would be to get plenty of rest and
nutrition. Dr. Mitra was having the nurses change their little rules for
me:

1) Do not disturb unless it's meal or medicine time
2) Change the sheets when I'm awake instead of waking me up to do it
3) Keep the door closed from the noise
4) Bring supplies regularly.

I finally stopped feeling like I was in an army barracks although I was still itching all over like a dog with fleas. And covered with Calamine lotion.

♪ When at night and I'm sleeping…
Jaundice itching comes a creeping… ♪

"I survived another night? Am I really still here?!"

I had to look in the mirror to make sure I wasn't a ghost! *{As I looked at myself, I decided to step on through this looking glass to the other side where I enjoyed briefly visiting the talking flowers in their beautiful garden.}*

I wrote in my journal my observation: "My body is tan with shades of yellow, especially bright and prevalent in my eyes, due to the jaundice. Urine is bright orange and stools are completely white. I'm a friggin' rainbow!"

Medically speaking…

- loss of color *(white)* caused by a lack of bile which is a digestive fluid produced by the liver, excreted into small intestine during the digestive process, and stored in the gall bladder.
- Jaundice *(yellow)* occurs when bilirubin builds up in the blood faster than the liver can break it down.
- Bright pigment *(orange)* is formed in the liver from broken down red blood cells

Newsflash! *The headlines in the day's paper said that 2,610 people died and 20,000 were admitted to hospitals in Bhopal due to poisonous gas leaking from the Union Carbide insecticide plant.*

It was the world's worst environmental disaster. It was so crazy in this country, a never-ending string of catastrophes! They told me that everything was normal, but everything ridiculous was normal! I wondered what would happen right there in Calcutta before and *if* I ever got out!

In the morning paper, the disaster of the day was: BOMB THROWN ON CALCUTTA UNIVERSITY. Elections were being held for a new cabinet, and one candidate had been assaulted and another killed by one of the hundred CPI supporters. They took their elections seriously. The famous actor, Amitabh Bachchan, had decided to quit movies and run for a seat in the parliament. He was the hero in the movie, *Sharabi*, which I had seen with the Polish girls.

Dr. Mitra walked in and gave me the bad news. The tests were showing *serum* hepatitis, which is a lot more serious and requires longer rest periods.

I decided to get as comfortable as I could (ha!) since I'd be staying a little while longer. There was nothing I could do but keep a strong will to be well. I began reading *Siddhartha*, a novel by Hermann Hesse that deals with the spiritual journey of self-discovery of a man during the time of Gautama Buddha.

I was continuously reading novels to keep my mind off of what was really going on with my life.

The same nurse who had forced me to give him blood the other day when I knew it was the wrong day, came again. He pulled out his rubber tube and syringe.

"Uh oh. You've got the wrong day again!" I said. "I am keeping tabs in my book."

He ignored me. I jumped out of bed and ran down to the nurses' station to tell them what had happened. They both assured me I was wrong, so I finally gave in. Later, when Dr. Mitra came in, I told him what had happened. He fussed at the nurses and told them I was right again. I knew it!

Dr. Mitra and I started talking, and he told me exciting stories from his patients. We shared funny and amusing situations and joked and laughed together. No matter how much pain I was in, he managed to put a little smile on my face. We established great rapport, and I realized that if I lived through the nightmare, this man was going to be my hero!

However, we got so caught up in conversation that he forgot to check my liver. I had to remind him. The test came back later that night, and my bilirubin had gone down from 7.6 to 5.8, but my SGPT, which indicates liver damage, had gone up from 110 to 130.

Later, alone in my room, I noticed the mosquitoes. The fan was on to swat them away. Now what? I thought, I'll probably get malaria on top of hepatitis. I was shivering under the cold fan, hoping I wouldn't get pneumonia, as well..*{The closer I looked at the fan, I realized that there was a large Cheshire cat sitting on one of the fan blades with a big grin on his face.}*

Meanwhile, there was a big commotion in the hallway; the patient next door in Room 408, from Assam, had hepatitis, too. He just died!. A number of women were crying in the hall. I was so frightened. I didn't cry since I was too busy praying!....... and singing...

♫ I gotta get outta this place...
If it's the last thing I ever do... ♫
(The Animals)

Then I started reading *Rich Man, Poor Man*. Even though my body had to lie there, I figured I might as well escape my predicament and run around New York City in my mind's eye. I quickly ate a meal and rushed back to New York. *(I wished)* Was this why my dear friends, Norman and Bill were always reading so many books? Escaping? In my situation, I called it keeping my sanity.

Soon, a nurse walked in and brought me back to reality.

I washed my hair and scrubbed my body but couldn't seem to get the damn yellow color off, especially out of my eyes. I stayed glued to my book, only putting it down for the three meals, tea time, Dr. Mitra's two daily visits, and medicine time. The books kept me still, which was what the doctor ordered. Dr. Mitra said to exert as little energy as possible, maybe dangle a leg off the side off the bed once in a while. Really?

Not much later, the florist walked in with a humongous vase of two hundred flowers from Delta Airlines. There was a beautiful card signed by the CEO and the President of the company (Garrett and Allen). The bouquet blossomed with red roses, carnations, lots of purples, long orange lilies, velvety burgundy and itsy-bitsy white ones. Following behind the florist was the district manager of Thai Airways, Mr. Nagara. He said he felt sorry that I had tried to go to his office eight days ago to try to get tickets to Bangladesh, but the flight had been full. (I didn't know it then but I had actually been very fortunate I didn't make that flight. I would have had to undergo treatment in Bangladesh if I had! Dodged that bullet!) The only reason I felt a need to go was because I heard it was worse than Calcutta, and I couldn't believe it, so I wanted to see for myself. Why did I feel this need? Curiosity killed the cat and it almost killed me.

Mr. Nagara said he wanted to escort me to the airport to go to Bangkok to recuperate further, since they had a cleaner and more modern facility. I was so excited that I sang him the Thai song that I had learned years ago in my favorite country of Thailand. He told me that when my SGPT reached 100, I could 'get the hell out of Dodge.' I felt like Siddhartha going from the depths of doom to finding Om.

I gave purple flowers to all the night shift nurses. Geno and Chanda took tiny yellow ones, but of course the doctor took a big rose. Isn't it funny how the little people take little flowers and big people take the best ones?

Friends that I had met along the way started to come visit me: Geno, Kamlish, Chanda, and Jali. Jali had been afraid to come visit me because he didn't 'seek to be a sick Sikh.' Wow, my mind was racing to throw that into a tongue twister. So I created this one:

> I sought to seek a shrieking sick Sikh in a shack at the Ashock, but I was shocked as he showed how Sheikhly he shot the sh_t, as he shook his share of dry sherry in a short shooter. Soon, I simply saw that it was none other than Shah Sher Shan Suri of Sasar.

I discovered that hepatitis is a great disease for people interested in dieting. No matter how much I ate—I was really stuffing my face—I didn't gain any weight. Even though I was just lying around! The calories just seemed to dissolve. My liver wasn't functioning properly and the food wasn't assimilating correctly. My metabolism was too high and the vitamins and calories were not being absorbed well due to liver malfunction. Too bad I couldn't get my liver to help me out when I pig out at a buffet. I could eat hot fudge sundaes endlessly! It could be a new diet plan: press a button on my liver to malfunction while I eat! And of course, the advertisement of it on TV would star Woody Allen.

CHAPTER 25

"No place is ever as bad as they tell you it's going to be."
Chuck Thompson

India – Calcutta (I'm outta here.)
Still in Belle Vue Clinic, it was a Sunday morning, but I was so 'sari' I couldn't make it to church. I thought maybe I'd take the day off and lie around in bed. My dad called, telling me he was worried about me. I felt sorry for my parents.

Kids are such a hassle. Are they really worth the trouble? One of the worst parts of my whole mess of a situation wasn't just about lying there miserably, but having my loving, concerned, wonderful parents worry. They feed you, clothe you, get you out of trouble in school, send you to college, try to lead you in the right direction, and spend their hard-earned money on you. And then they are helpless when you are ill on the other side of the world. I guess it must have been hard to have an adventurous kid who just wanted to run around to dangerous countries, playing with life, as if it's just a bowl of cherries. I obviously ate the wrong cherries this time, didn't I?

Susan called from the U.S. to check on me and cheer me up. She was a sweetheart, and told me not worry. *Hakuna Matata.* Thanks to Susan, my schedule and affairs back home were being taken care of.

I asked the nurses to tell me about my progress report, but they weren't allowed to tell me anything until Dr. Mitra arrived. So I snuck down the hall and waited until no one was around and peeked at my folder. I deciphered it myself and saw that my SGPT had come down to 85. Now I can travel at least to Bangkok. Dr. Happy came by and confirmed the good news. He was a wonderful doctor. My conquering hero!

I woke up the next day itching from the jaundice. I couldn't stop scratching. I needed a drink. Ha! My yellow eyes itched the most. If I didn't get malaria from the mosquitoes or pneumonia from the cold fan to keep away the mosquitoes, I thought I might scratch myself to death instead. At least when they cremate me on the Ganges, I'll have scratched all my skin away so it will burn faster. I'll need less sandalwood and ghee on the pyre, therefore, cutting the costs.

Nurse Das came in to bring me medicine for the itching. She was the sweetest one of all the nurses. I would have loved for her to work for Dad in his office. I thought that if I ever settled down and had a child, she could even come work for me. But then I didn't really think I could handle a 'mini me'—especially one that was adventurous, always getting into trouble, and somehow always getting out of it, too! Just like me!

The houseboy walked in to ask if I wanted lunch. He had been speaking to me in Hindi and required that I respond in it as well. He'd always start with *"Ab-a-cha-hay?"* (How are you?) And *"Nam ki-a-hay?"* (What's your name?)

All of my friends came by for the final farewell and Mr. McCall from the U.S. Embassy escorted me in a wheelchair to a waiting car to take me to the airport. I was exhausted from my sickness and wasn't sure if I'd make it. I remember wondering if this book would stop at 12/12/84, because it would be obvious that I *didn't* make it! I wrote this in my book in case it was found *after I kicked the bucket!*

On the road from the town to the airport, I saw more broken

shacks than I'd ever seen before. That was only a small fraction of the ten million people living in Calcutta. I was amazed when I saw that countless villagers had made their homes in huge tube pipes alongside of the road. It was their only shelter, and they built a community out of it. I heard it is worse near the railroad station.

At the airport, I was met with a wheelchair, taken through customs, and found out that the Thai Airways flight was almost full. Regardless, I was able to get on because my illness gave me priority over the other stand-bys. I was told *not* to look up and let anyone see my yellow eyes, as it was forbidden to travel with a contagious disease. I lowered my eyes.

Even though I had the most amazing experiences in India, I became choked up with mixed feelings of happiness and sadness. I was happy to be leaving after surviving my gut-wrenching experience. Yet I was sad to be leaving the kind, hospitable, caring people from this country that I had grown to love because I knew that I would never see them again. I would never be coming back. Even though I was silent, a gushing waterfall was streaming down my face. (My tears did not taste of salt! They tasted of *freedom*.) Mercy had reigned over my soul!

After my freedom flight, a Thai agent greeted me in Bangkok. He had a wheelchair waiting for me and escorted me to the limo. I went to Samitivej Hospital and ended up in Room 423. There was a TV, phone, radio, refrigerator, and even a balcony waiting for me. Dr. Thirdchai came to check me out.

CHAPTER 26

"He who would travel happily must travel light."
Antoine de St. Exupery

Thailand – Bangkok

Sawadeka! (Greetings)

Finally, I made it to Thailand. I was awakened at 6:00 a.m., but I threw the covers back over my head. They didn't kick me out of bed to change my sheets or force me to take vitamins, like the first morning at Belle Vue Clinic in Calcutta. The nurse just turned the light off, saying, *"My-pee-lie"* (No problem), and came back an hour or so later.

They wheeled me down the hall to take X-rays of my liver and they checked my blood pressure and temperature. I was told I needed to drink tons of coconut water and orange juice. My first meal was baked stuffed crab, asparagus, and other fancy dishes. Whenever I rang my call bell, instead of having to wait 15 to 20 minutes, four nurses appeared in five seconds. After arriving there, I think the Buddhas started watching over me, since everywhere I looked, I saw their statues. Someone from the Embassy called me and welcomed me to Thailand!

Newsflash: *Liz Taylor was doing it again for the eighth time. She found a nice Jewish boy from a quiet neighborhood—Dennis Stein.*

I wondered how long this one would last!

Dr. Thirdchai came by just to say hello and asked if I had any problems. I told him that I was still itching like crazy and complained that the Dom Pérignon wasn't chilled enough. Later, a gastroenterologist specialist, Dr. Kriengkrai Akarawong, came by. He was very kind and sensitive. I wished he was my regular doctor. *"My-pin-rye.'* ('Never mind') He told me that my pancreas was fine, and my gall bladder, too, and I was coming along well. I finally started feeling alive again! I had my life back? *Yes!*

My gourmet dinner arrived: chicken cacciatore, lobster with seafood sauce, delicacies de la mer, scalloppini, yaki soba, and pork orange flambé. It was delicious and healthy. They had hot water in the shower, and clean, white hospital gowns fresh daily. Everything was starting to...

♫ ...Come together... ♫
(The Beatles)

My dad called that night, and I told him I was still itching badly, so he said to ask the doctor for Periactin. He was always good at diagnosing and healing all of my problems, even long distance.

Watching TV: It was funny watching Joan Collins and Linda Evans speaking Thai on *Dynasty*. Also Miss Sweden was crowned Miss Universe.

I began reading the book, *Dreams Die First*, by Harold Robbins. Thinking back, I probably should have gotten the book, *1984*, by George Orwell because that was the year I started this journal. It was September 12, 1984.

The doctor came by and told me that all of my tests results were great. I was almost well! I knew I was getting better when I could stand in the shower without being out of breath. I felt like jumping up and down, screaming and dancing like my idol in college, James Brown!

♫ I feel good. I knew that I would now. ♫

However, I had to contain myself so I would not relapse.

Thinking back to my childhood, I remembered that Grandpa Jack named me, "Dynamite." How coincidental that my favorite entertainer would be James Brown, Mr. Dynamite himself! His amazing soul moves touched the depths of *my* soul. I had a life-size picture of him in my college dorm room, but my biggest thrill was to have him as a passenger three different times. All three times, we had our picture taken dancing together! He was always 'feelin' good!'

Dr. Akarawong came by to visit and told me I was well enough to go home, but I still needed more rest. I asked him if he thought staying in Thailand would be a good idea, and he suggested that Phuket Beach would be relaxing for a week or two. Oh yeah. He was my kind of doctor. (Note: I ended up staying in Phuket Beach for five relaxing and wonderful weeks).

The houseboy walked in with a beautiful huge vase of roses from Chiang Mai in northern Thailand. The manager of Thai Airways sent them.

Happiness is *not* waking up to a doctor staring at you. I slept late, packed my bag for the beach, and converted my traveler's checks to Bahts. I went to the airport hotel to get ready for my trip to Phuket. I realized that this was the first time I had been on the 'outside' in 26 days. I felt like I've been in jail.

I checked into a hotel for one night and went swimming at the pool. It was just what the doctor ordered. I felt so good that I saved a life. A beautiful multi-colored butterfly was drowning in the pool and I lifted it out and set it in the sun to dry. He was barely wiggling one leg. I thought the situation was hopeless, but after about an hour, he dried out, stood up, and finally flew away. This might sound really corny, but it made me feel good inside. I mean, after having had my own life saved, I was actually able to return the deed to another living thing. If

I hadn't fished him out, he would have died, for sure.

Sitting next to me at the pool, was an impressed Greg Hunter, Australian writer for *Penthouse*. He had traveled all over the world as well, so we had a very interesting conversation comparing adventures. In fact, he'd been barred from ever entering the Philippines again since he had written an article about their corruption, prostitution, drugs, gambling, mafia, and hoodlums. He read my notes about my own journey, and I asked him if there was any potential in making a book out of it one day. He said yes and was also impressed with my detailed descriptions. He normally had blond hair but had to put a black rinse on it when traveling to Arab countries. He taught me a lot about other countries' morés and attitudes.

I couldn't believe the number of countries that Greg had visited. We had swapped so many stories of our different adventures that night that when I got to my room, I passed out from jet lag!

After our encounter, I made it my goal to reach one hundred countries and thought maybe I could find a club for people that have done the same. Many years later, I actually found the Travelers' Century Club, or TCC, which is for people that had traveled to a hundred or more countries.

CHAPTER 27

"He who does not travel does not know
the value of men."
Moorish proverb

Thailand – Phuket

I took the early morning flight to Phuket (pronounced 'Poo-ket'). I was finally at the beach again, not to play in the waves, wind-surf, and scuba dive, but to relax and finish recuperating. I was told not to do any water sports!

The lush tropical island is 47 miles long with 100,000 people consisting of a mixture of Thais, Chinese, Malaysians, and Indians. Phuket is covered in rubber trees and coconut palms where white sands slope into the Andaman Sea. The islanders, who mainly stayed in the shade and seldom learned to swim, were amused that people would fly thousands of miles just to roast themselves in the sun and fill up with foods like lobster and spicy Thai dishes. Having traveled extensively in Asia, I fell in love with Asian foods and became one of those 'have chopsticks, will travel' sort of girls.

After arriving at Phromthep Palace Bungalows, I rented a little shack in Nai Harn Beach and relaxed in the sun. I was feeling wonderful with the sun, fresh air, and ocean waves. Just what I needed. There, I met Yves, a French garçon, who was traveling around for a year. His accent was beautiful, and I wished I could speak his language. I also met travelers from Germany and Günther from Liechtenstein. It reminded me of the tourists in Kathmandu, meeting from all parts of the world and becoming a family together.

Merry Christmas! I really enjoyed the holiday with friendly tourists from Switzerland, Australia, United Kingdom, and Canada. We all met for lobster dinner and watched *Bridge on the River Kwai* at our beach movie house. Once the lights went out, I read *Never Leave Me*, by Harold Robbins, by lantern. The place was a little community of unique, seasoned travelers, not 'drop-outs' like in Goa Beach. Harmony! OMmmmmm!

I made it a point to go to the telegraph office to make a call to Mom in the United States. She had recently read an article about how many people were dying of hepatitis, and it was becoming worse than AIDS. I told her I was finally out of the hospital and in a little village on the beach. My mother asked, "What the heck for?" I told her it was to regain my strength and that I had survived.

She was so thrilled and told me, "I'm glad you're taking time to smell the roses. Don't act like your usual self and overdo it." *Who me?*

Even though I had told my mother I was just lying around relaxing, it was a little white lie as I was starting to learn how to windsurf with another traveler, Vic, a back surgeon. I was pretty good, but Vic had to help me lift my sail up because it required a lot of strength, and, of course, I'm not supposed to be doing anything strenuous. There was nothing like gliding on top of the glassy water under a beautiful sunset.

The beach village was like being at camp again. I felt like a kid with no parents around. We did not have to go hiking or wake up early to pledge allegiance to the flag. What flag would we raise? There were people from about eight countries just in our little village. "It's a small world after all!"

After a delicious breakfast of coconuts, durian, papaya, and banana

pancakes, we all went snorkeling. It was a bit strenuous, breathing so long through such a small tube, so I didn't snorkel that long. We watched a beautiful sunset and enjoyed a New Year's Eve feast. The Thai guy in charge made a separate container of the punch without MeKong (Thai whiskey) just for me, since I was still recuperating. There was singing, drinking, and playing drums.

The drunkest of all was the Chief of Police. He loved my Thai song and had me sing it over and over again because he had fun singing it with me. The fireworks went up at midnight. I finally was able to spend a New Year's Eve in a foreign country, even though it took an illness to get me there. Some trade-off! Looking back, as I am finally sharing my adventures 33 years later, I have made it a point to be in a different country for almost every New Year's Eve.

CHAPTER 28

"Better to see something once than
to hear about it a thousand times."
Asian proverb

Thailand – Phuket, Pattaya

Sa-wat-dee bpee-mai. (Happy New Year!)

Everyone was recovering from hangovers, except me.

I tried to learn some of the Thai language. Günther spoke four
languages and was always trying to learn more Thai words. I memorized
the numbers: 1 (nung), 2(song), 3 (som), 4 (si), 5 (ha), 6 (hok), 7 (jet),
8 (bed), 9 (cow), 10 (sip)

For breakfast, I had ice cream and *durian*. It smelled bad but tasted
great. It's a cross between a pineapple and a mango with a yogurt-like
substance inside. However, papaya is the best of all fruits for the liver
and digestion, so I ate both.

I learned three new Thai words: *Teeruk* (darling), *mae loo* (I don't
know), and *na mo* (pig face). And lastly, some French words: *Ci dessus*
(above), *foie* (liver), and *grosses bises* (big kisses).

I woke up with right chest pain, but it was *ci dessus ma foie* (above
my liver). I didn't know if I should worry about it or not. I stayed in
bed and read my books on Japan and China.

After a short nap, I was 'good to go' again, as I just needed to
recharge my batteries. I had a delicious breakfast with Bruce and wife

Sonia from Brazil. Later, Günther convinced us to go hang out on the beach to play Jackets, a Lichtenstein card game. So, the four of us went to the Amusement Game Park, which was surrounded with white roses. *{The game, however, had been canceled because the Queen's Cards were too busy painting the roses red. So, we played croquet, instead, and our mallets were live pink flamingoes.}*

We decided to go snorkeling with the yachtsmen who had arrived. They took us to their million-dollar dive boat with a sunken bedroom. Inside was a king-size bed and plush wall-to-wall carpet. The owner, Ryan, treated us to a lavish lunch of freshly caught prawns and stingrays with North Malaysian *nasi kerabu* (blue rice from telang flowers), topped with bean sprouts and toasted coconut in spicy *budu* fish sauce. Ryan was a very happy camper. He had just recovered $6 million worth of porcelain from Malaysian waters while wreck diving.

Günther was in Thailand illegally because his visa had expired eight months earlier. He wanted to leave by ship so he could sneak out without paying the exit fines of about $1000. He was always smiling and laughing. He was a bit younger but I enjoyed his magnetic and humorous personality, and it was because of him that I put his little country on my bucket list.

We borrowed a motorcycle and went into the town of Phuket to call my mother, just so she would not worry so much. I told her I was with a guy from Lichtenstein and, in the faded conversation, she didn't quite understand. "Stein? Oh good, he's Jewish?" It was really funny. What a typical statement from a traditional Jewish mother!

Shopping for fruit and veggies to take back to the bungalow, we found *lamoot*, which is like a chocolate potato pudding. Yum! We cycled to Patong to find yachties with boats so Mr. Congeniality could work as crew. From Patong, we cycled home, singing all the way. Almost arriving at Rawai Beach, he told me what sharp eyes he had for driving at night, and all of a sudden... *CRASH!*

We drove right into a cement wall with a wooden chair set next to it. I was in shock, but Mr. Sharp Eyes was cool from the start. He lifted me up and pulled the wood from the chair out of my face. On the cement, there was a lot of blood but no guts. We had contusions, abrasions, and lacerations! Oh my!

But behold, a concerned Thai man came running and took us to his house. Would you believe he was the town doctor? What luck! Here it was 2:00 a.m., and the doctor had to get out of his bed and clean us up. I had to have stitches! I had a busted nose, ankle, hip, elbow, and knee. Mr. Safe Driver busted his wrist, elbow (protruding bone), hip, and calf. All of this cost Baht 170 ($7). What a stitch!

Wani-koon-sabaidee-roo-ka? (How are you today?) Our wounds finally healed, but our hearts were sad to leave each other. My dear friend found a boat in Patong and sailed away. So I went off to Pattaya for scuba diving. (After more than 30 years, I still have my souvenir scar on my face...and we are still friends.)

Pattaya

I arrived on the beach alone and met a Thai guy with a great big dragon tattoo on his back. I thought it was kind of cool, so I asked him where I could get one. Our conversation led us to learn that we both liked to dive, but neither of us had enough money to rent a dive boat. So we rented some scuba gear and paid an old fisherman to take us out in the water, and he dropped us off in the middle of nowhere.

The boy with the dragon tattoo was very macho. He said he didn't need a life vest or a snorkel so he went without. But after about 30 minutes in the water, his tank sprung a leak and he was out of air. He started screaming and tried to grab my regulator out of my mouth so he could breathe. I wouldn't give it to him because I knew it was not safe to share equipment like that, since he might not give it back to me. I didn't have an *octopus* (a second regulator attached to my tank), so all I could do was to take off my snorkel and throw it to him. He grabbed it and put it on, and that calmed him down. We looked around but there was no boat in sight. So there we were, stranded in the middle of the Gulf of Thailand. I thought this was the end. Again, right? We waited and waited, with nothing to even hold on to, with no land in sight, no cell phone (since they had not been invented yet). It seemed like an eternity, but the fisherman finally came back for us....Saved - one more time!

Travel Tip: Don't trust anyone with a dragon tattoo!

I managed to fit in Chiang Mai on an elephant tour as well as Chiang Rai to visit the Longneck Tribe, where I bought their scarves. They were beautiful, but flimsy and not very practical to wear, but I wanted to make them happy and buy their wares.

Okay, I finally decided to fit in Burma! Am I kidding myself? Was I really going to do this? With my health and all the pains I've been through? But...

♫ I haven't got time for the pain. ♫
(Carly Simon)

CHAPTER 29

"Life is either a daring adventure or nothing."
Helen Keller

Burma

Mingalaba! (It's a blessing!)

I was on my way to Rangoon. I had been told not to change any of my money on the black market, but I made my own decision because I could get 27 *Kyats* (pronounced "chats") for a dollar. In the bank, I would get only 8 Kyats for a dollar. It was a no-brainer!

I attended a Burmese/Chinese wedding in the lobby of our quaint hotel with delicious refreshments and music. I met someone to take me shopping to get a typical dress *(longi)* and monk's fan as I always dressed in the latest garb from wherever I was. Then we were off to visit the pagodas and the Reclining Buddha.

Next stop: Inlay. The kids were riding buffaloes, old men were running around, and women were walking with vases on their heads. I wanted to blend in but did not want to put a heavy vase on my head, so I just rode a water buffalo, wearing my longi, instead. They loved it!! I fit right in!

I felt like I was in an exotic and shocking place. It was the country I'd been wanting to experience, and I was very glad I was there. Inlay doesn't have the hassle and big city life of Rangoon. I could see the beautiful horseshoe mountains the country had been hiding behind,

the last refuge of an age-old lifestyle shielded for decades from Western eyes, finally opening its doors a little wider for the outside world to peak in.

After checking in at the Inlay Inn, I met Robin and Bubba from Romania, the home of Dracula. We took a walk around town, dodged buffaloes and greeted locals. Everyone, especially the kids, was so anxious to speak to the foreigners. A friendly girl escorted us back to the inn, and taught us how to count to ten: 1 *(tit)*, 2 *(nit)*, 3 *(thone)*, 4 *(lay)*, 5 *(nai)*, 6 *(chok)*, 7 *(ko)*, 8 *(shit)*, 9 *(go)*, 10 *(tesay)*. She also taught us to say thank you *(Jesu-timbadey)*. After a typical Burmese dinner, we watched the Pyisonn dance classical by candlelight.

A local girl invited us for tea in her house on stilts, so we joined her family, friends, and even pets. *{There were so many exotic characters, I felt like I was at the Mad Hatter's tea party.}* They gave us chai and veggie balls. The people were beautiful, friendly, and polite. Inlay Lake is nine miles long, and we watched the leg-rowing fishermen. Our first stop was at the Floating Market at the Inpaw-Khon village where we watched Inlay silk being woven on hand looms and village folks in their dugout canoes selling fruits. I bought a cool shirt to match my longyi. We took a bus to the wooden pagoda where we just mingled with all the monks.

Next stop: Pagan. The beautiful city has four million pagodas within 16 square miles of each other. It is the richest archeological site in all of Asia and is situated on the eastern bank of the Irrawaddy River. Pagan dates back to 109 A.D., and attained historical greatness in 1044 A.D. under King Anawrahta. Since then, Buddhism has flourished. Pagan has become the seat of Buddhist learning and the center of Burmese culture.

Our driver, Maung Maung, and tour guide, Aye Aye, picked us up in a horse and buggy. We all sang Burmese and English songs for each other into my cassette recorder while they drove us to a thatch-built guesthouse to meet other travelers. We got together to climb the most famous pagoda at sunset. The most darling little girl, Maw Maw, led us with a flashlight up the dark steps to the top where others were sitting. We all watched Mother Nature create the most gorgeous bright red sky streaked with pink. Can you imagine?

At that time, Burmese law only allowed tourists to spend one week there, so I made sure to take advantage of every moment I was there. I woke up every morning at 5:00 a.m. in an eerie darkness of dawn to watch the sunrise at a different pagoda. A blinding ball of fire was rising into the multicolored blues of the sky. At the pagoda, there were huge golden Buddhas, some sitting and others reclining. Paintings were plastered across the walls to depict their history. The tour that Mo Mo led cost 15 Kyats/hour, which was only 50¢ on the black market. I took time to shop at the lacquer shop and bought a bowl made from entwined horsetail! Each shop served Chinese tea

with *jaggery*, sugarcane balls, plus a
dish combination of tea leaves, nuts,
and ginger. It tasted great!

Next stop: Rangoon. My next
flight took me back to Rangoon, as
one must exit the country from there.
I visited the Shwedagon Pagoda. It
is over 2,500 years old and 326 feet
high. Magnificent Buddhas in a gold
interior filled a circular room that was centered around a gold dome.
As usual, everyone was smiling and pointing toward me, as I was the
only Westerner wearing their traditional longyi. They loved it when I
spoke in Burmese and said *"Mingalaba"* (Hello) and *"Jesu-timbadeh"*
(Thank you).

> ***Travel Tip:*** Please take the time to learn to say hello and
> thank you in the local language. You will get smiles of
> happiness that you bothered to take the time to care.

After sunset, something bizarrely interesting happened. Throughout
my travels, people have asked me to take a photo of them with me. They
gave me their addresses and asked me to send the photos. A young boy,
Phang, at the pagoda wanted the same, but since I was out of film, he
found the 'tourist-photo-taker,' paid for photos to be taken, and asked
for my address to send *me* one! What a pleasant change, eh? Well, I did
give him my address, and he actually sent it.

On the way back to the hotel, the driver pulled over to get lighter
fluid from the gas tank. He attached a tube to the tank, gave it one
suck, and got it flowing so he could put gas in his lighter. What a great
trick! Was that a travel tip?

Those were seven great days in the land of golden pagodas. I could never feel free as I was always changing money illegally and rushing around to see everything in only one week. It was like I was in an immense, beautiful, tropical paradise of a jail. Burma has an authoritarian military junta government with too many restrictions, but the people are some of the friendliest I've ever met. I do believe that their women have the most beautiful faces in the world. After looking at various photos in shops, I realized there are numerous tribes of people all over but in remote areas that I didn't have time to explore.

Speeding forward, you really never know what will happen next in a land ruled by an authoritarian regime. Just four years after my first venture in Burma, an uprising by the student populace almost toppled the regime and caused massive crackdowns for years to come. Interestingly enough, I just happened to be back there in 2011, coincidentally four years after a second attempt at a revolution. This time, the pacifist Buddhist monks headed the revolution, and, unfortunately, everyone suffered the same fate as the first revolt.

On a more positive note, since my last trip to Burma, there have been significant shifts toward democratic reforms, and it seems that the days of dictatorship may have finally come to an end. Incidentally, the one-week restriction limit on visiting has also been cancelled.

CHAPTER 30

"Nobody can discover the world for somebody else.
Only when we discover it for ourselves does it become
common ground and a common bond and
we cease to be alone."
Wendell Berry

Philippines

Kamusta! (How are you?)

I finally realized it was time to start my journey home and I figured the best route would be to go through Manila. Once I got there, I stayed at the Swagman Hotel, which was surrounded by strip bars with erotic dancing. I took a taxi, a bus, and a ferry just to get to Puerto Galera Island where I met a group of Germans. We all went to White Sand Beach by Jeepney. Two of the guys wanted to pick up Filipino girls; they called them *Flip chicks*. However, they were afraid of picking up something else as well, and they weren't sure if they wanted the free gift. After a motorcycle ride to check out the town, we went to Don Leo's Disco. The two guys met some girls (at 150 pesos/night, $7.50). They were very cordial with sweet dispositions, and we had a truly memorable evening talking and laughing together.

I spent the day hanging out on the beach with local Filipino kids, taking photos, and taping songs on my recorder. I gave the kids plastic souvenir airline wings, and they gave me free mangos and bananas.

Such a deal for me, right?

> ***Travel Tip***: Throughout my travels, people have been
> thrilled by the little gifts that I bring to them, from 'pigs
> to the Pope.' I gave little presents to locals everywhere, and
> even the Pope in Rome. *Read on!*

The German group showed up with a bottle of Tanduay, local
Manila rum. (Personally, I stuck with mango and *guyabano*, a local
Manila juice.) That evening, the locals killed a pig, skinned it, cut its
insides out, and roasted it. It was gory to watch but great to eat. In spite
of not being very kosher, we enjoyed a fulfilling feast. The belly and
neck tasted the best, and the head was saved for 'Mama.'

I headed to the airport for my final flight back home to the U.S.A.!
Not surprisingly, there were many hassles. Philippine Airlines wouldn't
take my ticket because it was written to Honolulu, and the only flight
going out was to San Francisco. Japan Airlines didn't have a good
connection. Korean Airlines couldn't get the manager to rewrite my
ticket because it required a visa. China Airlines would write it but not
until the next day because it was Sunday. Then I tried to contact Pan
Am, but they wouldn't even answer the phone. Nothing could be done
at the airport, so I went back into town.

I was running out of pesos so I picked a cheap hotel to check into.
The newspaper on my bed stand told of crime, brutal stories, theft, and
bloody ordeals in what was considered Sin City. Nuns and religious
schoolgirls paraded down the street, singing in protest against the
smut, prostitution, and crime on Pilar Street. Roaches were crawling
all over my things. Yuck. I had to get out of there.

Philippine Airlines came through. I was finally on my way home
to Atlanta, Georgia. The four elderly women seated next to me became

my best friends for the flight. We couldn't communicate well, but we sang and laughed together. I was laughing the hardest since I was *ultimately* on my way home! Relief at last!

After five months of chills, ills, running up bills, mountains and hills, kills (goats in Nepal, Gandhi in India, crime in Manila) and pills, I'm still alive and *not* needing a will!

Here's to civilization, health, clean streets, phones that work, freedom from rodents and roaches, no ridiculous social and sexual morés, decent transportation, hot baths, drinkable tap water, *not* spitting betel nut, no more bargaining, good postal system, pepper-less food, washing machines, and my family.

After learning a bit of Urdu (Pakistani), Nepalese, Hindi, Thai, Burmese, and Tagalog (Philippines), the one language I tried hardest to learn was French from the French travelers. Wouldn't it be a dream come true to return to work and have the company pay for flight crews to learn French in the French Riviera? Oui, oui! What a concept! Then, I could marry a spicy French chef/baker and name our daughter after Brigitte Bardot!

♫ As dreams that you dare to dream really do come true. ♫

So ends my complete circle around a remarkable world. My past journeys had taken me from the U.S.A. to another continent and back, but I was adamant about circling the globe this time. I would start from the U.S.A., cross the Atlantic Ocean to Europe, continue onto South Asia and then the Philippines in the South China Sea, and return by crossing the Pacific Ocean to return to the U.S.A.

From the delights of Prohibition of Pakistan, to the shocks and enchantments of Nepal, to the splendor of rags, riches, rapture, and rapture of India and the Philippines, and the smiling faces of Thailand,

I wouldn't have wanted to miss a bit of the experiences I had. Even my devastating illness was a story in itself. I went through a lot of hellacious drama but also reaped heaps of unbelievable magic and incredibility, which made all the hassles worth it. It has been such a golden journey! Cheers! I finally did it. Whew!

♫ Somewhere over the rainbow,
bluebirds fly...so did I! ♫

Part 2

DEEPER DISCOVERIES

Having finally returned home from this incredible adventure, I saved the notebook that I faithfully wrote my stories in every single day for five months starting on September 12, 1984. I put it in a drawer and sort of forgot about it, as I was so busy trying to get my life back together. That was 33 years ago.

I realized that I've had so many more monumental and meaningful experiences—crazy, dangerous and off-the-wall voyages—in many other countries since then that I wanted to share more of my adventures with my fellow 'travelers.' You!

So here goes!

CHAPTER 31

"Travel is the only thing you buy that makes you richer."
Anonymous

France

Bonjour! (Good day!)

Several years later, my wish came true: my airline obtained the route to Paris. They offered in-flight crews to take one month out of the three available months to go to Juan-les-Pins on the French Riviera to learn the French language. I went to the base manager, Jackie, and talked her into giving me all three months.

As I attended classes, I realized that the girls who were learning French the fastest had all met boyfriends who didn't speak any English. So I found Jacques! Voila! Not only did I become fluent in the beautiful language, but I went on several excursions with him. One of the best of them was going to the Grand Prix in Monte Carlo, Monaco and meeting Prince Albert II.

By the time I returned home to Atlanta, I had become fluent in French and realized that I hated having to speak English again. I found a group that got together the first Wednesday night of every month. They held potluck dinner parties with lots of music and dancing. It was a mixture of French and Americans together.

As it happened, I was looking for a roommate at that time, so I went up to the podium, took the microphone, and announced it in

French. I asked for a *'compagnon de chamber.'* Everyone laughed at me and told me that I had asked for a 'companion in my bedroom'! They told me that I needed to say that I needed a locator, and the word for that is *'locateur.'* My new friend, Alain, moved in the next day, and he could not speak a word of English. I was thrilled!

A year later, when Alain started picking up a little southern English, the first words that came out of his mouth were, "Have a nice day" in a perfect southern drawl! It cracked me up.

Alain was a baker and brought home scads of chocolate croissants. I immediately gained 20 pounds. He made the most delicious pastries, onion bread, cakes, pies, baguettes, and more. We had many common interests, and I felt that he was *Le Petit Prince* for me. The ceremony took place on the diving board at our condo pool. After our vows, we took the plunge in all our clothes!

One day, a few months later, Alain said to me, "Une vie sans enfants ce n'est pas une vie" (A life with no child is no life) so we started working on making our lives more of a life! In fact, I checked my very organized calendar and realized it was a 'fruitful' day for me: Oct. 20, 1987. So, I canceled my beauty parlor appointment and opened the champagne.

Exactly nine months later on July 14, 1988, Brigitte was born, exactly 199 years after King Louis XVI of France was overthrown at the Bastille, on July 14, 1789, French Independence Day!

> *Note*: If a French citizen has a child born on French Independence Day, that child is awarded a present from the French government.

We often visited my French in-laws in a small country village of Domqueur, France. Alain's family was made up of farmers and gardeners with chickens, sheep, cows, rabbits, and ducks. His father was a sheepherder. I instantly fell in love with his down-to-earth, kind, and fun-loving family. Each person has a great sense of humor and everyone is always laughing and joking.

My husband had also inherited some farming techniques from his family. We started with tomatoes and our efforts grew into a gigantic garden with 37 different fruits and vegetables.

One of our neighbors had a bird, and so we decided that perhaps we should try to breed them too. Even though Alain had never bred birds, he thought he would give it a try. He read about how to breed cockatiels so we bought one male and one female and allowed them to 'boogie.' When the female hid in the corner of the porch in our bird sanctuary, and moved her hips back and forth, we knew she had laid the egg. We counted 19 days for hatching; right on time, we heard the little baby peep, and we removed a tiny, pink, featherless dinosaur-

looking creature about two inches long and put it in a makeshift nest that Alain had fabricated.

Instructions:

1. Get a large empty coffee can.
2. Inside, put a hot rock bought from a pet store. (Plug it in.)
3. On top of the rock, put a square Kleenex box with a paper towel in it to catch any droppings.
4. Put the baby inside the box and put it in a dark corner of a closet away from any noise.
5. Using a syringe, feed it with the thick liquid baby bird formula every three or four hours.

We named our first baby bird Rose, after my great grandmother. We continued to breed these cockatiels until we had eight of them. We clipped a bit off of one side of their wings so they couldn't fly. They would walk around like any other pet. When the wing grows back, it can fly again.

Digressing for a moment, I remember many years ago when my sister Carol and I traveled to France to learn the language. We were offered a two-week trip to stay with a farm family for one week and then with nobility in a chateau for a second week. Because we were

having so much fun with Carol's friends those two weeks, we got side-tracked and missed out on visiting the farm family. Having French in-laws who were country folk later gave me the opportunity that I had previously missed.

But I need to tell you about the week we spent with the Count and Countess de Viller. Every night, we had a formal dinner with our hosts and were served the most extravagant eight-course meals on beautiful china with sterling silverware. We were each given several glasses: one for aperitif, one for red wine, and one for white wine. The custom was to drink the apéritif and nibble on hors d'oeuvres for 30 to 45 minutes before the real dining experience began. At that point, we would decide which wine we would drink according to what we had just eaten and what would suit our palate.

Travel Tip: Learn to drink wine properly like royalty.

When I returned home, I went out to dinner with a friend. Instead of the usual bottle of wine to share, I ordered three glasses right away—one aperitif and two glasses of wine (one white and one red). My friend thought I was a little bizarre so I explained to him the above travel tip and my short exciting life in the luxurious chateau. *A votre santé! (To your health!)*

A startling event occurred while Carol and I were in France. One morning, we looked at the French newspaper and read, LE ROI EST MORTE! (THE KING IS DEAD!) We were wondering which king had passed away; France didn't have a king! Maybe England? As we arrived at the beach, we saw a lot of sad faces and some people crying as we heard the song, "Love Me Tender" playing on the loudspeaker, and we realized which king had died.

Since I was French qualified with Delta, I enjoyed many Paris and Nice trips. I attended the Nice Jazz Festival 2001. I could not see the entertainers, since the festival was packed with people. But being my daring self, I climbed a tree to see. Well, of course, I fell out of the tree. The security guards and First Aid team ran to my bloody rescue. They cleaned and patched me up, but, danger over, nothing was broken! I must have a guardian angel. I had to hang on to my friend's sturdy arm for the rest of the evening.

A funny thing happened in Paris on a layover. I decided to fool the crew and be a smart aleck, so I wore my blue burqa from Afghanistan over my uniform, and boarded the bus before the rest of the crew. When they came down for pick up, everybody was afraid to get on the bus because they thought I was a terrorist and had a bomb under my burqa. The bus driver told me, "Lady, this is not a public bus. You must get off." I threw off my burqa and surprised everyone. The scare was over, and they laughed because they were so relieved.

CHAPTER 32

"I travel a lot; I hate having my life disrupted by routine."
Caskie Stinnett

Africa

Jambo! (Hello.)

This journey began in Kenya. Roommates, Mimi and Joy, and I took an airline special with TWA for $100 round trip! After photographing the wild animals on safaris, we had the utmost pleasure to visit a Maasai warriors reserve and join in their dances. Being in my early twenties and not having read about them in advance, I thought it was all a big show. At that time, I couldn't believe this still existed. Little did I know what was to come in my future travels, as this book relates.

The natives welcomed us and were intrigued by Mimi's platinum blonde hair. They had never seen anything like it and began to run their hands through it. I'll never forget her crazy giggle and the look on her face because she knew they were covered from head to toe with a mixture of red clay and cow dung! (Fortunately, the portable video camera had been invented a week prior to our arrival, and we were able to get this all on tape.) *Hakuna matata!* (No problem)

A few days later, we went to the local African airline company to fly to the beach of Mombasa on the Indian Ocean. Sharks, whales, dolphins, stingrays, and sea snakes and other fish all live here but do not come up on the beach, fortunately. The airline turned us away,

even though they were not full.
They said to return the next day.
We were upset but could do
nothing about being left out.
It was all very fishy. That night,
on the news, we heard that the
plane had crashed into the sea
with no survivors! Very fishy!

Speeding forward for a
comparison: Many years later, I
took my daughter to meet Maasai warriors, but in Tanzania. The queen
offered to buy my daughter for her son for twenty cows. Wow, such a
deal.

On the safari, we were almost attacked by elephants while we were
in the jeep too close to their watering hole. I was sitting in the front
seat and was petrified. I shrieked and dropped my camera.

The driver was nervous and immediately put the jeep in reverse as
we backed up a few feet. The African land elephant can be the most
dangerous animal to humans on the planet, especially if you block the
path to their waterhole!

At night, we slept in luxury tents with our own private bathroom,
but we had to have one of the local helpers pour water in a hole at the
top of the tent to be our shower. I do not like to wake up early in the
morning and be chilled before sunrise, so I thought of a solution. I gave
our souvenir coffee mugs (from the shop at our last lodge) to one of the
helpers that prepared the coffee in the morning; I gave him a nice tip
to bring us hot coffee at 5 a.m. as they have to get up at 4 a.m. to begin
the days' preparations.

Travel Tip: Take an insulated cup to give to the houseboys the night before to fill it with hot coffee in the morning. Not only does it warm you but it serves at an alarm clock. I had to pat myself on the back for that one!

When we visited one of the schools, the kids sang, *'Jambo'* (Hello) for us in Swahili. We loved this adorable little song. I learned it and have had fun singing it with the Africans that have spread out all over the world, even our Uber drivers.

I never thought that I would be visiting Nigeria, but my girlfriend Cherýl had her wedding in Lagos. She timed it perfectly on a two-day layover, so not only was the transportation and hotel free, we were attending a wedding and phenomenal party, and making money all at the same time. This is a specialty of airline crews. This could be called multi-tasking?

It was very interesting to see all the African ceremonies and rituals involved. It was a very soulful ceremony, and the bride said I was full of soul and I was the only white girl invited. I was an honored honky! One ritual was throwing money at the feet of the married couple as they danced. A little flower girl with a small basket came around collecting the money thrown at the bride and groom. Everyone starting throwing money at my feet, as well, just to show acceptance when I joined in dancing! However, I had to pick up my money by myself. Aw! What a chore!

During another layover in Africa, I thoroughly enjoyed viewing Cape Town. We spent a full day of shark diving. The captain lowered me into the water into a cage, and it was astonishing to see these massive mammals up close and personal, circling the cage looking for their next meal. That experience is etched in my memory for life. Cape Town has one of the most exotic botanical gardens I have ever seen in a natural setting. Kirstenbosch is nestled at the foot of Table Mountain. It has the most interesting and varied plants and flowers imaginable, little land penguins and monkeys roaming around unattended and breathtaking views.

Next, there was an excursion of Robben Island to the old prison where Nelson Mandela was incarcerated for twenty-seven years for standing up for civil rights for black South Africans. While we were taking the tour, several of us had to use the restroom. There was not one in sight except for a toilet in Nelson Mandela's prison cell. The toilet had a DO NOT TOUCH sign on it. I waited until the tour passed on, ran back, and climbed over the rope into Mandela's cell and used his. Not to be disrespectful and break the rules, but my bladder was about to burst. Whew! Saved again!

CHAPTER 33

"A journey of a thousand miles
must begin with a single step."
Lao Tzu

China

Nǐhǎo! (How are you?)

Many years ago, (somewhere in the 1970s), my first visit to China was to Hong Kong. As Red China was still communist and a forbidden territory, we were allowed to take pictures of it only from the border, while standing at the edge of the China Sea. With my face pressed against the binocular lenses, I stared across the water of this heavily monitored border, intrigued by the huge picture of Mao Tse-tung.

Years later, when China did finally open its doors to the world, my passion and wanderlust was lit like a piece of dynamite! I studied the history, geography, culture, and language, and planned a five-week tour that would cover all of Red China. It would include a night train to Inner Mongolia, including ten days in Tibet and a quick stop in Japan on the way home. But first on my agenda was to climb the Great Wall in Beijing. *{As I sat on the wall for a photo, I met Mr. H. Dumpty from England. He, too, was sitting on the wall. But, I didn't really have much opportunity to talk with him, as he fell off!}*

In Shanghai, there was hardly anything but dirt roads, and transportation was mainly by bicycle. There were very few cars. Biking

down a dirt road, I was practicing a very well known song, *Tian Mee Mee* by Teresa Teng. I had acquired a knack for learning songs in the countries I visited, and I had become proficient at memorizing them.

On this day, I kept forgetting what came next in the middle of the song. Knowing that it was a classical, popular song, a light bulb went off in my head. An old lady a few feet ahead of me was on her bicycle with a young boy sitting on the handlebars. I pedaled up really close. I started to sing 'Tian mee mee, nee- shouda tien mee mee...' I got to the line that I was having difficulty with, and she heard me falter, as I did it three times, looking at her with a question mark in my eyes. To my delight, she joined me and picked up exactly where I had left off, and we continued the whole (very long) song in tandem, pedaling down the dirt road together. It was a magical moment I'll never forget! (This is a highlight of solo traveling.)

One might say that I *'shanghaied'* this lady to help me! (Sadly, Shanghaied local peasants were kidnapped for labor on crew ships before World War II in the days of prostitution and opium addiction.) The city was also known as 'The Big Lychee' as it was the largest city in Red China.

When I visited Shanghai 30 years later, it had become a kaleidoscope of neon lights, restaurants, clubs, sightseeing, and impressive world-class shopping. This hub of modernity also houses centuries-old shrines dating back to ancient kingdoms.

Inner Mongolia

I joined a group of Chinese tourists, and our entry into Inner Mongolia was unforgettable, to say the least. Our group had been traveling by bus, and we had just approached the entry point. We had reserved an overnight camping site and it was critical that we make it across the border to get there before nightfall. The bus came to a stop, and when I looked out of the window, I saw we were surrounded by at least ten evil-looking men with rifles. The leader, looking mean and surly, stood in front of the bus with a long, thick rope. The group denied us entry, saying that the roads were flooded and no one could get in. What were we going to do? After being parked there for about half an hour, I

finally went up to the bus driver to ask a few questions.

"What's going on here?" I said.

He responded, "The locals won't let us through. They're saying the roads are bad, but that's not true."

"Wait, what do you mean?" I confusingly asked him.

"They are just pushing their authority on us. They just don't want to let us through. They just want to order us around like a game," he said.

I asked him, "Are you sure?"

"Yes, positive. I have the weather report," he exclaimed.

At that point, I knew I wasn't going to let them intimidate or bully us. I also knew they had weapons, and there was no telling what they were capable of doing.

A surprising boldness came over me. I got off the bus and walked up to the leader. I gave him a gracious smile and started talking sweetly, knowing that there was a language barrier. But I continued to talk to him softly, and simultaneously, I gently lifted his right arm and moved it to release the rope that marked the border. I didn't know what he was going to do next, but to my astonishment, he actually raised his arm and finished releasing the rope for us. I shook his hand and thanked him repeatedly with a huge smile. I kept thanking him and began backing away to get on the bus. (I didn't feel like being shot in the back that day.)

The driver wasted no time crossing over, and I told everyone to wave and blow kisses to show our gratefulness, and they smiled and waved back. What a miracle! After my heart stopped beating so fast, I realized how a smile and soft sweet voice works in every language.

We arrived at the camp, which had huge yurts to sleep in. A yurt is a circular domed tent of skins stretched over a collapsible framework. After an authentic Mongolian BBQ, the Chinese taught me how to play mahjong that night, Chinese style! I actually liked it better than the American style since there is not a card of choices to follow; you must create your own strategies. The game originated in China during the Qing dynasty, and there is a legend that the philosopher Confucius invented it. During the next several weeks of traveling through China, I was able to participate in the game with the locals. It was a terrific highlight of my journey. Who needs a cell phone when you have mahjong?

CHAPTER 34

"Wandering re-establishes the original harmony
which once existed between man and the universe."
Anatole France

Tibet

We continued into Tibet, the 'roof of the world.' Lhasa is located
12,087 feet above sea level so before we could venture out, we had to
breathe oxygen for 45 minutes.

Travel Tip: Do not ignore this personal experience tidbit; it
will prevent you from suffering from altitude sickness. The
hotel to pick is one that has oxygen attached to the wall in
the bedroom. So, do your homework. (This is an amazing
country to visit when you are young and in good health!)

I aimlessly wandered alone into a monastery full of chanting monks. They offered me a mat on the floor to join in, and I enjoyed the melodious chanting and spiritual energy for the next hour or so! I was overwhelmed with this inspirational exposure. I had chosen the right path. It was just the monks and me!

I met three lovely women selling turquoise jewelry. It was all very stunning and I wanted something meaningful. I loved the earrings so when asked which ones I would like, I pointed directly to this woman's very own earring in her ear. She was shocked but flattered and kindly gave it to me. The reason I wanted that earring was not to just buy a souvenir but to have this memory.

To go to a famous monastery, we had to take a truck, then a boat, and then another truck to finally get there. The complicated route was well worth it. Inside the monastery, the art along the tunnel walls was amazing.

> *Travel Tip:* When visiting the monasteries, the light from the yak butter candles is minimal. So if you want to do justice to the gorgeous paintings along the tunnel walls, bring a pocket flashlight! I did! (Or, if you have a smartphone, you're covered!)

 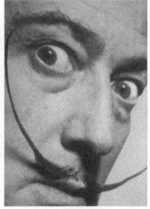

The entire time we toured the area, children would constantly run up to us, asking for a picture of His Holiness, the Dalai Lama. This is because all images of him had been banned since his exile in 1959, so most children had only rarely seen actual photos of him. (The Dalai Lama was always my favorite doll, next to Salvador Dali, that is.)

> *Travel Tip:* While on the subject of altitude sickness, do NOT go straight to Bolivia. The major city, La Paz, is 11, 913 feet above sea level. Instead, cut down on elevation problems by making a stop in Peru to see Machu Picchu or Colombia to grab a cup of coffee (or coke or emeralds) on the way there. I wish someone had given me this travel tip! Bolivians are fun loving and fascinating, but when your body feels sickly, even after you have continued to drink heaps of coca tea, why bother to be there? Remembering my discomfort, I won't even tell you about it right now. Maybe it will be in my next book. (That's the sequel that will also contain all the porn I took out of this book!)

Japan

Konichiwa! (Good afternoon!)

On the way home from China, I thought I would check out Japan. I heard that the hotels were expensive, so I thought I would stay only one night. After I arrived by train in Tokyo, but before I had a chance to inquire about a hotel, I saw a long-haired backpacker walking by. So I ran to catch up with him and asked if he knew of a place to stay that was affordable. He looked at me and said, "Follow me."

We rode the bullet train together to Kyoto, a city located in the central part of Honshu. He led me to a Japanese-like hostel where everyone had their own space, a futon mat to sleep on, and a locker, all in one gigantic room. We shared bathrooms and the kitchen, and it only cost $5 a night. I had an instant family to enjoy breakfast with and instant friends to join with for touring around. It worked out great. I was alone to follow my heart and I didn't have to talk a travel partner into following this guy! I stayed an extra eight days, just to explore.

There were lots of classical Buddhist temples, gardens, and palaces to visit and many delicious Japanese cuisines to divulge in. One night, I was invited to go to one of the nicest Japanese restaurants, where we picked our fish out of a pond. The fish was so fresh that when my friend poured his beer into the fish's mouth, it gurgled from the beer. Now that's fresh! When he asked me what country I wanted to see next, I told him that I wanted to go home, get married, and have a child. He taught me a children's song to sing to my unborn child called 'Po-Po-Po'. I sang it to my daughter all the time when she was still *in the oven*.

Shopping Tip: Japan has the best miniature electrical 'TENS' units. The unit has two pads attached to place on pulled muscles, aches, pains, and arthritis. The unit fits in your pocket, and you can keep moving instead of lying on a table. Why waste time going to a chiropractor when you can buy your own for $50 and heal as you go?

CHAPTER 35

"Stuff your eyes with wonder,
live as if you'd drop dead in ten seconds.
See the world. It's more fantastic than
any dream made or paid for in factories."
Ray Bradbury

Panama

One interesting destination during the mid- to late-1980s was Panama. I arrived toward the end of Manuel Noriega's military dictatorship, which was in fact propped up by the United States Central Intelligence Agency. Noriega's rule was a rather strange twist in the long and convoluted history of U.S.-Latin American foreign affairs. The CIA installed Noriega, a long-time informant, as a sort of puppet dictator in 1983 to maintain its unquestioned control of the Panama Canal. Much to the dismay of the U.S., the canal was due to be handed over to the control of the Panamanian people. This would never do, so Noriega was put in place.

All the while, Noriega trafficked in narcotics and human misery, which was well known and documented by his CIA handlers. At some point in the mid-80s, Noriega went rogue and stopped obeying his orders from the CIA. That prompted the 1988 U.S. invasion of Panama as a means of ousting Noriega after his crimes had become too numerous. The entire event turned into an international debacle and blackened the eye of U.S. foreign affairs in Latin America for many years to come.

So naturally, I found myself smack in the middle of all this and more.

While all of this was going on, I managed to enjoy a trip down the Panama Canal to the indigenous areas and found wonderful silk for my dining room curtains. I found them at a fourth of the price and better quality than could be found at home, dictator be damned.

> *Travel Tip:* Visit the orchid farms to see some incredibly beautiful flowers. My favorite, the Dove Orchid, is endemic to Panama. It is white with a miniature dove inside of it with eyes and a yellow beak. Next time you look at an orchid, take a closer look inside it.

CHAPTER 36

"I haven't been everywhere, but it's on my list."
Susan Sontag

Germany

Guten tag! (Good day!)

It was November of 1989, and one of my more educational encounters occurred during a long layover in Frankfurt. I hopped on a quick flight to Berlin to help make history. The Berlin wall had stood as a barrier separating families and loved ones for almost 30 years. The wall was a symbol of the ideological chasm between the capitalism of the West versus the communist philosophy held by our enemy in the East, the Soviet Union.

After Ronald Reagan declared, "Mr. Gorbachev, tear down that wall," I found myself standing at the base of the Berlin wall with hammer and chisel in hand. I was wearing my Santa suit as I had been shopping for the holidays. Mass protests by the East Berliners had debilitated the Soviet puppet government's capabilities for maintaining control. The barrier that had once seemed so insurmountable was being chopped down and everyone was invited to join in! Naturally, being a Westerner in Berlin for such a historic event was a once-in-a-lifetime opportunity, so I seized it with the vigor of a true capitalist.

Since I was able to recover broken pieces of the wall, I returned to the U.S. with a large bag of fragments of history that I knew would be

Taking a little time off from my normal Christmas shopping to help chop down the Berlin Wall with my hammer and chisel.

worth preserving. Sitting in the middle of my kitchen floor on top of newspaper, I took sections of the wall and coated them with shellac. I then broke them into smaller pieces and crafted earrings, necklaces, even pendants. It was a very profitable venture, indeed, and everyone at home was thrilled to have a souvenir slice of history!

I attached them on my business cards with the words, WEAR THE WALL, and charged $20 a pop! I guess my capitalistic tendencies were instilled as a child by Grandfather 'Pop.' He was a true entrepreneur, with a love for creating poetry and telling his story. I guess I inherited that too!

At this point, I need to pay tribute to my finest passenger of all times. Now I promised myself that I was not going to recount airline situations in this book, or tell about my wild layovers, especially in Vegas with Redd Foxx, Billy Joe Royal, and Brenda Hogan. That was taken care of by my dear friend, Casey Grant, in her fabulous historical book, *Stars in the Sky: Stories of the First African American Flight Attendants,* which I highly recommend! In my book, however, I just want to show the fun and perks of traveling almost free all over the whole globe. I am breaking that promise in order to pay tribute and respect to Dr. Siegfried Heyden from Germany.

I was working in business class, which included a large number of seats, a small kitchen buffet, and a smaller section of ten seats, on a flight to Munich. When I realized that there were about 10 empty seats in the main portion of business class and only one person in that small section, I asked Dr. Heyden if he would like to move forward with the rest of the passengers. At first he said "No." He told me he was still upset over a problem with the last flight he had taken on Delta and he just wanted to be alone. He had a horrible scowl on his face. He seemed quite distressed.

I invited him to join the rest of the guests and promised him that I would see to it that he had the best of care. I said that we were sorry about his last flight and that I personally was going to make him happy to be with us again! I told him that I would be his special attentive stewardess for the next eight hours. He agreed. I could see a glimpse of hope in his sad eyes.

I began by making him comfortable with his blanket and pillow in a seat by a window with an empty seat on the aisle. The crew worked a fabulous service for all the passengers, but for the entire flight, I was Dr. Heyden's personal servant. I was there for anything he needed, and we had marvelous conversations during the flight. It so happened that he had written a book similar to one that my father had written. He gave me his book, which described how he and his father hid Jewish people from Hitler during the Holocaust in Germany. I promised to send him a copy of my father's story, which I did.

At the end of the flight, he said it had been the best trip of his entire life, and that he would always fly Delta if there was a stewardess like me. He melted my heart! He wanted to keep in contact, so we swapped information. As he deplaned, he had a magnificent smile on his face.

For the next five years, he called me and wrote letters to me. Every time he had a flight back and forth from Germany, Italy, and Zurich, he asked me to work those flights, and I did! I worked the flights that his wife travelled on, too! She brought me presents of her art. I developed a wonderful friendship with Dr. Heyden. He even invited me to come for an all-expense-paid vacation for a week in Germany (on a tour he was conducting) with my daughter for my birthday. I accepted. My daughter was thrilled since she was studying World War II in her history classes at her school. He was 96 when I last heard from my dear friend, Dr. Heyden.

I recently called his daughter to tell her I have included a story of him in my book, and she confessed to me that sometimes he would take a trip just to see me. How sweet and touching. Memories of kindness and caring like these, I will cherish forever from my Delta career.

I have to admit, the times that touched my heart were when I had passengers in distress and I was able to solve their problems.

CHAPTER 37

"If you can't live longer,
live deeper."
Italian Proverb

Italy

Buongiorno! (Good morning/afternoon!)

During my flight to Italy, I befriended a nun who was Mother Teresa's main confidant. I asked her if she knew how to sing like the nun in *Sister Act* and before I knew it, we were singing together! We were having such fun that we started exchanging travel stories and were impressed with each other's adventures. She then took off her necklace of Mary, put it around my neck, and said, "Mother Teresa would love for you to have this." I felt so honored! Then she gave me the phone number of Father Foley in Rome as my connection to the Pope.

Father Foley met us at my hotel. I gave him presents: two souvenir watches in the shape of Delta airplanes that I had bought from our duty-free shop. One was for him and the other one was for the Pope. I was honored, especially being Jewish, with front row seats for the crew to the Sunday Mass, referred to as the Papal Audience at the Vatican! Oy vey! It was an inspirational experience of peace. Afterward, our visit to the Sistine Chapel, painted by Michelangelo, was completely over the top! (Well, it is actually *under* the top!) I never needed to take a vacation in Italy, since I toured a number of locations on different layovers: Milan, Lake Como, Florence, Venice, Cinque Terre, and Tuscany. Of course, I learned two Italian songs, one of which Dean Martin taught me...Volaré.

Malta

Even though the Vatican is known as the smallest country in the world, according to *National Geographic*, the Order of Malta (in Rome) is actually the smallest sovereign territory in the world. They have their own stamps, passports, and currency, and unless you were born there, you are not allowed to be a resident. So, I decided not to miss it. It was behind a black iron gate, and I had to plead with the guard to let me in just to take a picture and say that I was able to set foot there and check it off my bucket list.

Been there! Done that! But no T-shirt!

Austria

Zdravo! (Hello!)

Working with an airline has so many perks that we started flying five-day trips to Austria and that gave us three days in Vienna to simply play around. I can attest to the fact that I ran all over seeing all the museums, and they were some of the most amazing ones I have ever seen in my life. But after three or four trips there, I was ready for something else. I decided to take a trip and conquer another country, Czechoslovakia, right next door, but none of my crew wanted to take that chance. It was like that box of chocolates: you never know what you're gonna get or what could happen.

CHAPTER 38

"Tourists don't know where they've been,
travelers don't know where they're going."
Paul Theroux

Czechoslovakia

So I took a flight to Czechoslovakia, as, at that time, we did not have that route. I became friends with other travelers at the B&B in Prague. We toured all day together. That night, in a quaint little restaurant, everyone ordered what they wanted to eat and drink and then the waiters brought each person their own bottle of free wine. How did that happen?

I took a train from Prague to Bratislava where I bought gorgeous crystal wine glasses that I had shipped home. Delta did not fly here, yet, so it was a shopper's paradise for me since everything was so expensive in Vienna, including the famous cuckoo clock.

The scary part of this jaunt happened when I went to the airport to board the flight back to Vienna. The airport was fogged in, so the plane couldn't take off, and all flights were cancelled. My heart started pounding when I thought of the possibility of losing my job. I tried bargaining with a taxi driver, and he said he would charge me $400 to take me back to Vienna. Just as I was about to succumb, the fog lifted, and it was announced that the plane was able to fly to Vienna. Saved again!

Little did I know that I would be adding two countries to my list from my little trip, instead of just one. That's because, years later, Czechoslovakia divided into the Czech Republic and Slovakia. Two for one!

Ireland

Top of the morning to ya!

The most intriguing aspect of Ireland was its green rolling hills (with wandering fluffy sheep and leprechauns), especially on the way to Blarney where I just had to *kiss* the Blarney Stone at the castle. (I actually put my finger in between the stone and my lips, as I'm sure there are lots of cooties from zillions of tourists doing the same thing.)

I visited a social club in Dublin, and it was announced over the microphone that an Irish dancing competition would take place the following week. I thought it was an amazing idea to enter the competition, but I was better at clogging than Irish dancing, so I wondered if I could pull off an even crazier idea. (Years ago, I had actually taught jitterbug-clogging in Marietta Square.) I came back the next

My daughter in Irish Dancing Group

week with my clogging tap shoes. I entered the contest, held my hands down, and fists clenched like an Irish dancer, and I clogged instead, high kicks and all. The judges had never seen this before, and I won. When questioned about my dancing and where I was from, I said in my southern drawl, "♩ I come from Alabama with a banjo on my knee. ♫ And that's how I do it back home."

Dominican Republic

I took a vacation with my family and we went to Punta Cana. One day, we were on an excursion that included swimming with the dolphins with a group of other families. When it was time to get into the water, a little boy started crying because he would not be allowed to go into the water and ride a dolphin since he did not have an adult to accompany him; his mother could not swim. My daughter, Brigitte, who had been swimming and diving since age two, went over to the boy and invited him to come with her. He was absolutely thrilled and so was his mother. I could not have been more proud of my precious little girl.

CHAPTER 39

"Travel is rebellion in its purest form."
Anonymous

Russia

Zdravstvujte! (Be in good health!)

The first day I spent in this country, I danced the traditional Cossack dance in front of the famous St. Basil Cathedral. In the market, I met a striking young man, Sarmat, who helped me bargain. Then he invited me to come to his house and dine with his mother. I fell for his line. We were driving at night, and it seemed like it was turning into such a journey, that I started feeling a chilling sensation. Maybe he was kidnapping me and taking me to some faraway place to steal my money and then dump me out! How could I be so gullible and trust someone I had just met in the market? At the height of my nervousness, he finally slowed and pulled up to a little house. The next thing I knew, we were eating caviar, drinking vodka, and singing Russian songs with his mother! *Ya tebya lyublyu.* (I love you.)

I visited the Kremlin and saw the intricate Fabergé eggs and the elaborate gold chalice collection of the ancient czars, and I could not even believe the wealth I was witnessing. (A chalice is a very ornate drinking goblet.) I was reading a book about Nicholas and Alexandria as I traveled through Russia and I felt like I was actually a character in this book. (This is a travel tip to enhance your appreciation!)

I saw so many things at bargain prices that I ended up buying huge amounts of Russian matryoshka dolls, fur hats, jewelry, and local crafts. They made wonderful presents.

Morocco

Salam! (Peace!)

Sherry tried to force me to go to Morocco with her. I got nervous when she told me that we would be spending the night in a tent in the middle of the sand dunes and riding camels in the desert at the crack of dawn. But I finally agreed to go and I was so glad that I did. She chose a tour company that was safe and took care of our every need, so I felt better. The only thing wrong was that our tour guide was observing Ramadan and could not come into the restaurants with us, because he was fasting and didn't want to be tempted. That meant we didn't have an interpreter. And since the only languages spoken in Morocco were French and Moroccan-Arabic, all of us on the tour began to get frustrated and tired of having the same meal of basics like couscous and tagine chicken.

By the third day, I couldn't take it anymore. I finally asked the waiter, in French, if we could order other meals besides the standard ones.

"Bien sur (Of course)," he said.

So, I did!

I saved the day! As our companions were well-educated doctors, lawyers, and businessmen, I felt important and respected to be able to achieve what they could not. My self-esteem soared.

One evening, Sherry and I befriended a young local man who invited us to dinner at his house. We were privileged to be able to break the 'fast' of Ramadan with his family and enjoy many fun-filled hours in their home.

> *Travel Tip:* Have an open heart to experience deeper joys in traveling by sharing rich traditions in each culture. Get yourself on the inside, instead of just observing from the outside.

CHAPTER 40

"The world is a book, and
those who do not travel read only one page."
Saint Augustine

Poland

Ceść! (Hello!)

Instead of telling the story of Poland from my personal adventures, I'd rather let my grandfather, Abraham, take the stage.

He had written about his life and had given his writings to his son Joe, (my dad) 50 years ago. Dad was sad (I've seen it in his eyes) that he had never had a chance to do anything with Pop's writings since he was always so busy doing his own thing. So he gave the writings to me in hopes that I would do something meaningful with them. He told me that he hoped that a little part of this kind, humorous, and loving man would not fade away and forever be forgotten. So I've included a small part of the story of his life and childhood, one hundred years ago, in his own words:

"I was the youngest child in a family of three children: Charlie, Anna, and me, Abe. We were the children of Joseph and Elke. We lived in a small town called Yanova, and we owned a very large watermill. We grounded the grain of rye and milled the wheat into white flour for the people who brought us their grain to be processed.

They would come in horse and buggy from as far as five miles away and sometimes have to wait two days for their turn in line for their grain to be put in the hoppers and processed. As a young child, I always admired those who could perform manual labor, but being so young I was not allowed to do so. Charlie operated the slicing machine that would cut up straw and alfalfa used for the animals' food. One day I was watching him operate the machine. I got too close and my shirtsleeve got caught in the slicing gears. Charlie grabbed my arm at the last minute from the machine; my arm would have been sliced off in the semi-circle of slicing knives. I suffered from 12 bites, but it finally healed and I survived.

"To get permission to go to the U.S.A. was not easy and was filled with many papers and spending months in an emigration camp controlled by the Germans. It took a couple of years to get over all of the red tape and multiple delay problems. I was finally transferred to Southampton, England where I boarded the ship, the S.S. Teutonic, owned by the White Star Liner company. I spent the next 12 days on board and my accommodations were in the lowest and smelliest part of the boat of what was called the steerage cot. I only had a brown paper bag that held all my possessions in the world! I finally arrived in New York City, but my relatives were in Mobile, Alabama, so, after more delays, I took a trip on a ferry boat and a three-day train to finally arrive in Mobile with smelly boots, no money and no English language!"

A short time later, the same company built another ship, the famous Titanic! If my grandfather had been delayed any longer, he could have easily been on that ship. It was the exact same company, *The White Star Liner,* and the exact route he took from Southampton to New York City. That was April 15, 1912, when 1,503 perished!

That means that this little book might never have been written! Not only did I adopt his love of writing poetry and stories and his love for being an entrepreneur, but I also inherited his love of swimming and diving, and his knack of being saved from imminent danger. A coincidence: As these writings were handed down 50 years ago, my book also goes back to almost 50 years when I started my flying career.

Here's more from Pop:

"After *finally* arriving is this blessed country, I was faced with the problem of making a living, and I ended up in Camden with Charlie and wife Rose and brother Henry. As there were no jobs for a poor fellow like me, my brothers put some merchandise in a pack to carry on my back, go out into the countryside of farm homes and try to sell my wares door to door. After many exhausting journeys like this, I finally made enough money to buy a horse and carriage to avoid having to walk so many miles. My broken English: 'Please look see if anything you like... my price cheap.' The local people always were kind to me and let me sleep in the barns on the corn shucks, fed me a tasty supper and gave water to my horse.

"The next job I had was flushing chimneys and spreading hot tar on leaky roofs. It took a week to complete one job and I was paid $3, so I rushed to the store to buy pants for half my wages. My happiness inspired a little poem:

The pants with side buckles of brass
Latest style for real manly dress
Really nice and nifty
The price, a dollar fifty

"My next job was in a pawnshop and I received $25 a month and meals with the family. Finally, my brother-in-law sold his horse and buggy and bought a car. We took pleasure rides with family and friends. I enrolled in the Y.M.C.A. and became very well known and popular for being religious and quoting from the Bible. I finally was able to open a little grocery store with living quarters upstairs, so, I sent for my main squeeze, Minnie to come to America. We married, put our hearts and souls into the business and did very well.

"I added a new line to our business as there was a great demand for horse feed. We had room for stocking feed and bales of hay. We were very popular, as the city installed a trough for the horses to drink at no cost to me. This helped our business a great deal! We even got a maid, Irene, and the going price then was $3 a week. Not only did she clean and cook but was very protective of our new son, Morris. He was the sweetest little boy and increased our happiness. Then came our second child, Arthur, who was always full of laughter! Soon after, Ethel was born and two years later we had Little Joe. At five years old, Joe could read. All his buddies from kindergarten came to our porch with the newspaper funnies spread out, their behinds up in the air, listening to the escapades of Chester Gump, Cicero's Cat and Little Orphan Annie.

"As the years passed, Ethel got married at a very early age and all three boys joined the army, where Joe became a medic...and later a physician. In 1953, we sailed to England to visit Minnie's relatives. On the boat, we met a family from Atlanta, kin to Margaret Mitchell, (of *Gone with the Wind* fame)! We arrived in London with perfect timing. As our son, Arthur had married Rita, we were also able to visit her mom and Dad (Pat and Zen) in Liverpool. My grandchildren, (Beth, Michael and Johnny), were visiting, as well.

"A week later, a monumental opportunity occurred that was also perfect timing that we were there: We witnessed the multitudes of people in raincoats sitting in tiers watching red coated horsemen trotting and leading a four horse-drawn carriage with a hand waving from an open window. We were elated to be involved in this historical event, the actual coronation of Queen Elizabeth II at Buckingham Palace!"

(As Pop was watching the Queen's coronation in majestic color, I remember, as a little girl watching it as well, but in a cheap apartment on a small black-and-white TV on Monterey Street in Mobile!)

Note: Since I am praising my Grandfather Miller, I need to mention Grandfather Gurwitch, on my mother's side. Jack Gurwitch never left any writings about his life, so I can only mention what I can remember as a little girl. He was kind and very loving, and he named me 'Dynamite' as a child. He always brought me M&Ms, and therefore, I can blame that addiction on him. Whenever I feel distraught and depressed about anything, I always buy M&Ms and think about him. I guess the reason that works is because it's just a mentality that changes my karma. But, it does work! My mother loved him so much; we were persuaded (forced) to give Brigitte the second name of Jaclyn.

In summary, because of Jack's mother, my Great Grandmother Rose, we have three celebrities in our family: Janet Gurwitch, fashion and cosmetics entrepreneur in Houston; Annabelle Gurwitch, famous author and television star in California; and Maury Gurwitch, TV advertising guru from Hattiesburg, Mississippi.

CHAPTER 41

*"When setting out on a journey,
do not seek advice from those who have never left home."*
Rumi

Guatemala and Costa Rica

When I realized that the best way to learn a language was to immerse myself in a country that speaks that language, I decided my next endeavor would be to learn Spanish. I visited Guatemala with the lively colorful markets and the famous Mayan Tikal ruins with Mirna, my local *amiga* from the Spanish school. I also saw the magnificent volcanoes in Costa Rica and went zip-lining through the forests famous for their many tropical birds.

> *Travel Tip:* Stay with local families and enroll in a language school. It is also less expensive than hotels.

I was able to go on educational excursions on the weekends with my host families or other students from the school. In fact, the *abuela* (grandmother) in my Guatemalan home was madly in love with Ricky Martin and was always salsa dancing to his music all over the house. Both families I stayed with were delightful. By the way, grandmother's cooking was fantastic in her tiny kitchen. Whenever she would make black beans *(frijoles)*, she served them as beans; the second night, they became softer bean soup; and the third night, whatever was left became a mush-like paste to eat with chips. Delicious!

CHAPTER 42

*"There was nowhere to go but everywhere,
so just keep on rolling under the stars."*
Jack Kerouac

Argentina

Buenas tardes! (Good afternoon!)
When I started flying to Buenos
Aires with Betty, my favorite
dancing pal, we took Spanish, salsa,
and tango lessons. When I took a
month off to study Spanish there,
I would spend many nights doing
the tango so late that I would miss
my Spanish lessons.

One day, walking down the
touristy Florida Street, I heard
beautiful music. I followed the
sound and came across Raymi, a
street performer, who was playing
the pan flute. I was so impressed
that I started looking at the CDs
he was selling. He asked me if I
would like to buy one, and since I

could speak the language, we were able to communicate. I said Yes, but only if he would teach me how to play the pan flute. We planned to meet at the lobby of my hotel and he began to give me lessons. I took the pan flute home and practiced, and when I learned how, I played it with him on the streets.

♫ No llores por mi Argentina ♫
(Don't Cry for me Argentina)!

I guess I got this urge from my father because he played the harmonica. I surprised myself with some of the crazy things I did, but a little craziness once in awhile prevents permanent brain damage, right? Because of that incident, I became friends with him and his family and we had many amusing times together.

Chile

My layover partner-in-crime, Kat, and I were in Santiago, Chile, where our favorite seamstress lived. Rosita sewed all of our clothes with perfection and charged only a tenth of the price we would pay at home in the United States. Not only were we being paid to go to amazing Chile but we were also saving a fortune in seamstress fees as we lugged all our clothes to her. To top it off, she and her husband were fun party animals, so we went out dancing! (multi-tasking again? you better believe it)

One day, there was a demonstration over the soccer stadium being torn down. Kat and I were in the middle of the crowd when it started getting tear-gassed. We fell to the ground, gasping for breath, and getting pounded by the force of a water cannon. Luckily, there were some friendly, young Chilean boys who carried us to our hotel.

CHAPTER 43

"The first condition of understanding a
foreign country is to smell it."
Rudyard Kipling

Mexico

Hola!

Many, many years ago, I had a layover in San Diego, and I decided to
venture into Tijuana, Mexico. As it was the late 60s, it was that time in
history where everything was 'Flower Power! Peace and Love Brother!'
I bought a very huge Buddha made of white cement. I decided to
paint it gold when I returned home and sell it for a profit. I bought the
statue for $3, paid a sweet little Mexican boy to carry it over the border
for $2, and he put it in my waiting taxi. The hotel porter put it in the
baggage room, and the pilots put it on the plane, a DC 8, and strapped
it into first class! I sold it for $100 to one of my Bohemian friends. I
was onward bound to success. *Muchas gracias, amigos!*

Turkey

Merhaba! (Hello, there!)

My favorite bargain story occurred in Istanbul. My friends and I had
just been to the Sultan's Palace and the enormous Grand Bazaar, and we
were headed to the Topkapi Palace. A teenaged boy selling a gorgeous
prayer rug approached me. I asked him how much it cost, and he said

$100. I said, no, but he kept following me and said $90. I said, no again, and he continued to lower it to $80. It was no again. Just as we were finally entering the doorway of the palace, he had continued to lower the price and it was $5. I turned, smiled, and said, "Okay. Perfect." I handed him a $5 bill. The rug was silky and gorgeous, but, with my best poker face, I pretended that I wasn't interested. (You gotta know when to hold 'em...know when to fold 'em) I figured that my tactics were going to succeed when he started going lower, but I didn't know his price would go that low. He was trying to scam me, but after all of my traveling endeavors, I have become a scam-master!

Travel Tip: Be careful in taxis when you pay. The Turkish lira is worth only about 33 cents to our dollar, so their money has many zeros and is confusing. For example, you will give the driver a bill of 200,000, but he will swap it quickly and show you that you only gave him 20,000. This is a very common trick played on tourists. Take heed!

The most amazing highlight of my trips to Turkey was the time I bought so many gorgeous pashminas when people in the U.S.A. did not even know what a pashmina was. (It's a fine-quality long scarf made from goat's wool.) Then I began to find them in China and India for even lower prices.

As I traveled to other countries, I went crazy with bargain shopping and I found:

Alpaca capes, sweaters, gloves, hats, and ponchos from Peru

North Face jackets, Uggs boots, designer purses (Coach, Chanel, Bottega Veneta, etc.), pearls, silk scarves from China

Dead Sea care products from Israel, containing therapeutic minerals

Electrical TENS units from Japan, to relieve muscle aches

Columbia jackets from Taiwan

Assorted silk clothes, Disney socks, personalized luggage tags, and neckties from Korea

Scarves from Chiang Mai, Thailand

Shoes and socks for Irish dancing from Ireland (my daughter and I were in an Irish dance group)

Gorgeous housecoats from Dubai and Kuwait

Electronics from Hong Kong

Wine and cheese from La France.

My dear friends Margie and Kathy took advantage of the opportunity to purchase and sell jewelry from all over the world. Even though it was Margie's merchandise, Kathy was a darling and was always organizing it for various holiday sales. She took care of every detail with her heart and soul like it was her own. Kathy was always the greatest true friend you could ever hope to have in your life—kind, happy and caring, a true angel!

CHAPTER 44

"Your wings already exist.
All you have to do is to fly."
Anonymous

Korea

Anneyeong haseyo! (How are you?)

I shopped all day at Itaewan for unbelievable bargains: everything you could imagine. The real fun began, however, when all the shops closed. I had befriended one of the shopkeepers, Yunmi, who had a gathering every night for some of the vendors in the other shops in the market. Everyone brought a different Korean dish and spread them out on a large plastic tablecloth on the floor. (Like we did in Pakistan and Afghanistan, remember?) There was plenty of delightful spicy food to go around.

There are 800 ways to prepare kimchi, so we enjoyed a few of these varieties along with many other dishes. Kimchi is definitely an acquired taste, so I simply had a little of it every time I was in Seoul, and I started to love it! Of course, there was plenty of *soju* (distilled from rice, barley, wheat, or potatoes) to go around, served by her husband, the village dentist, Dr. Chung. One of the favorite dishes was the little octopus, *sannakji*. When served, they are still moving around, their tentacles stretching in and out! *Really!!* You dip them in sesame oil to avoid having them stick in your throat. Everyone was Korean except me, but I was accepted as I could say many things in their language and could sing three different local songs with them.

Peru

Hola!

After having been enamored by the gold museum in Cuzco and the breathtaking views of Machu Picchu, I felt just as thrilled to ride the llamas in the countryside. One of the nights in Lima, there was an earthquake. It started all the way from Pisco, trembling the ground for over 130 miles.

Alpaca model, Jenny

Pieces of the walls were falling into the bedrooms, forcing people to evacuate the building. However, I never felt anything and did not try to escape. I found lots of little pieces of the walls all over my suitcase. I was still alive when I was told of this occurrence. I had slept through it, as I had too many Pisco sours!

My favorite tidbit to share about this country is the Magic Water Show in the Parque de la Reserva, the fountain spectacle in Lima. When searching for the greatest fountain in the world, I found a delightful one at the Bellagio in Las Vegas; second best for me was the splendor of the music in Arabic, English, and French at the Burj Khalifa in Dubai. But my number one choice was the Parque de la Reserva in Lima with five fountains shooting upward at different times, one right after the other. It was a laser show of rainbow colors as Michael Jackson and Elvis Presley and other pop icons were reflected singing and dancing in the beams on the water. *Magnifico!*

CHAPTER 45

"Broad, wholesome, charitable views of men and things
cannot be acquired by vegetating in one little corner of the
earth all of one's life."
Mark Twain

Egypt

Marhabaan! (Hello!)

My daughter, Brigitte, and I took a cruise down the Nile and did the
whole tourist thing, including riding camels and climbing pyramids.
But when we went to a grand private party in our hotel, I had a little
trouble. I couldn't help but take pictures of the glamorous ladies there,

dressed so sexy in short dresses that showed plenty of cleavage, and dancing provocatively. But a guard came up to me and explained that they were considered religious women who normally wore *nijab* in public so that men would not get sexual ideas. A *nijab* is a black dress that covers a woman from head to toe and has only a small opening for the eyes. The guard grabbed my camera, removed the film, gave the camera back to me, and said a few things that I dare not repeat.

Israel

Shalom! (Peace!)

I am infatuated with this amazing and amusing country. We floated in the Dead Sea's healing minerals, went scuba diving in the Red Sea in Sharm Al Sheik, (which was owned by Israel at the time) and hiked the ancient ruins of Masada. We shopped in the Carmen Market in Tel Aviv and bought freshly squeezed pomegranate juice, gigantic fruits and vegetables, and the absolute best hummus dip.

But, it was in Jerusalem where we visited the marvelous Chagall Windows at the Hadassah Medical Center. The light that emanated from the stained glass bathed the Abbell Synagogue in a special glow. Marc Chagall, a Russian-French artist, created them to represent the Twelve Tribes of Israel. The local rabbi, Mordecai, told us not to take pictures there. I had heard that it was a trick to make us buy their postcards in the souvenir shop, so we decided to out-trick them. We were running low on shekels (Israeli currency), so we used our spy camera. While my friend aimed the camera at me, the lens was turned sideways, capturing the view on the side of the temple. We captured photographs of the famous Chagall windows!

Then we went to the Wailing Wall and prayed for atonement because we had broken the rules and taken the pictures!

Shalom Aleichem. (Peace be upon you.)

CHAPTER 46

"We wander for distraction,
but we travel for fulfillment."
Hilaire Belloc

Spain

A memorable event occurred when I was in Barcelona with my spirited friend Kat. After spending time at the supernatural Sagrada Familia Basilica, by architect Antoni Gaudi, and the mind-blowing Salvador Dali Museum (who is my favorite artist of all time), the two of us enjoyed ourselves at a nightclub. As we walked back to our hotel through the Plaza Square, we noticed a sleazy character following us. He tried to start a conversation with me.

"Why are you talking to a stranger?" Kat asked me.

"Because I am practicing my Spanish," I answered.

All of a sudden, the man grabbed my small purse out of my coat pocket and pulled my chain from around my neck. I was very upset because attached to the chain was a small globe, which was my favorite piece of jewelry 'in the world.' To me, it signified my ambition to travel around the world.

I was enraged, and I guess my karate skills kicked in, since I instantly turned and gave him a brutal karate kick in his abdomen. He dropped my necklace and purse but I grabbed them as he fell to the ground. All of a sudden, the police showed up and overtook him. I had to let them

drive me to the jail so I could fill out a report. I took the report back home the next day, gave it to my sidekick, Hurricane Emily. As her parents were from Ecuador, she could translate the Spanish to the class. Everyone was proud of me! Emily and I had been practicing karate together with our two daughters, Brigitte and Chrissy, to get our black belts.

Brazil

Oy!

Having been to Rio and São Paulo numerous times and having had terrible seats to the famous yearly carnival, my girlfriend Marcia told me to come and visit her, and promised that we'd have great seats for the event. To my surprise, when she picked me up at the airport, she told me the sad news that we did not have tickets after all. Disappointed, I asked her why not. She laughed and told me we didn't have the tickets because we were going to be in the carnival! We danced our booties off in the parade. Marcia always surprised me with outrageous gifts. (A year later, she hired Andrea Moreira, samba dancer from *Dance Brazil*, and her husband Todd on drums, to entertain at my Beach Blanket Bingo Birthday Bash.)

Switzerland

Guten abend! (Good evening!)

One of the happiest, safest, healthiest countries in the world is where my friend Vreni lives: Switzerland. We met years ago when we studied French in Chateau Laval on the French Riviera. Vreni's language was Swiss-German and mine was, of course, English. We realized that we both had the same high spirit and we were both always ready for adventure, but due to our language differences, we couldn't communicate. So we both studied extra hard so we could speak in French. She was so funny that I wanted to call her a turkey, and she said that the Swiss translation would be a 'crazy chicken' or *'verrücktes huhn.'*

Years later, I visited her, and we enjoyed the Swiss costume carnival called *fasching*, cheese fondue, and skiing in the Swiss Alps. While on

the long rides on the chairlift up the mountains, she taught me a Swiss song. I learned the whole thing except I could never grab onto the yodeling at the end. She could yodel perfectly! During one trip, she drove me to Liechtenstein. It was like a small village, so we saw the whole country in one day!

We've kept our friendship for 20 years. The last time I visited her, we had a *raclette* dinner (a simple meal made of melted cheese and bread) with her husband and two grown children. Vreni said she had a special Swiss present for me. I was thrilled until she presented me with a big red Swiss army knife! I could not accept it since I wouldn't be allowed take it on my flight. I laughed and told her that by giving me a weapon before a flight, she was the real *verrücktes huhn!*

CHAPTER 47

"To awaken alone in a strange town is one of the
pleasantest sensations in the world."
Freya Stark

Vietnam

"Good morning, Vietnam!" *Xin chào!* (Hello!)

Sherry and I toured the Chủ Chi tunnels, the immense network of
the Viet Cong that were used as hiding spots for combat during the
Vietnam War. The tunnels served as communication and supply routes,
food and weapon caches, and living quarters.

Our bus tour took us through beautiful scenic spaces where we saw
women in the paddy fields transplanting rice seedlings. Our tour guide,
Hang, asked if we wanted to help. Being curious and always striving to
learn and experience more about cultures, Sherry was so excited that
she jumped off the bus, tucked her dress up, and waded right into the
water! She was the only one that took her seriously. The group on the
tour bus could not believe their eyes and snapped pictures like crazy!

Travel Tip: This is where one can find the best ginger chips in
the world. The older ladies sell them in big bags on the street
and also in the markets.

Here's another travel tip: This is the only country I have ever been to that reveres two dollar bills as good luck when praying to the Buddha statues in their temples. So when you're bargaining, show the merchant

that you will be paying with your credit card or cash but that you will also be using a two dollar bill; they will be thrilled and let you bargain down to a lower price than it would be normally. It was funny to see their eyes pop out when they saw a $2 bill.

One of the girls on the tour, Cammy, was actually native to Vietnam, so, to my delight, she invited me to go home with her to meet her family. We rode on motorcycles with her cousins to her house, dodging the tourists. I rode with Hoang the Nguyen. He was fun and hospitable, and his wife and two children were precious. I enjoyed this rare opportunity as well as one of the best meals on the trip. At dinner, we toasted to happiness and our hearty meal with the local beer, (Bias 33) *The toast: Mo^.t hai ba do^*

> *Travel Tip:* As a tourist, someone calls out "sticky rice" as the group huddles together to cross the street, dodging the motorcycles!

Laos

Sabaidee! (Hello!)

I was awake at 4:00 a.m. in the quaint city of Luang Prabang for the centuries-old tradition of early morning alms. I chose my spot to sit on the side of the street as the monks, dressed in their orange robes, came by for the offerings. We held containers full of rice ready to scoop into their bowls. Even though it was a very serious ritual, I decided to break the rules, and I snuck a few candy bars into my bowl. The monks that received the candy gave me big smiles, even though they weren't supposed to show delight! So, they broke the rules, too! I was thrilled because I felt guilty for being mischievous.

Later that evening, on our way back to the hotel, I could hear singing and music, which made me curious. I said to another traveler, "Hey it's early. Let's go check this out!" She looked at me with surprise and said there was no way she was going to go out in the dark unknown when we were so close to our safe hotel. So, nervously, I went by myself and walked a few blocks to find the source of the sound.

I came across a group of about fifteen teenagers who were having a feast and playing several musical instruments. They sat around a huge plastic tablecloth displaying at least 20 different exotic foods. One of the young boys asked me where I was from. When I told him, the USA, they all cheered and asked me to come join their party. They started playing American songs so that I could join in. They showed me the traditional way to eat Laotian food. You simply take a chunk of sticky rice with your fingers and use it to stick to the vegetables, meat, or other items you would want to put in your bowl. Once you had two or three choices in your bowl, you would eat them with the sticky rice. Then you would go for another round with different items. It was delicious and one of the best meals I had the pleasure of sharing.

Cambodia

Chomreabsuor! (Hello!)

There are 1.5 million people in Phnom Penh and 1.3 million mopeds. They are everywhere. Unfortunately, one night there was one too many on the road for me. As I was riding in a *tuk-tuk* (an open wagon pulled by a man on a bike) to a market with a backpack on my lap, a young thief came by on his moped and snatched it from my lap. There was no way we could chase after him after he sped away. My driver started screaming, and I did, too, thinking about all of the important things I had in my backpack. I calmed down when I remembered that I had put my iPhone in one pocket of my pants and my money in the other. So what did he get? Nothing. Just an empty backpack that I was on my way to fill up at the local market. Travel Tip: I recommend that you always remember the Three P's rule: **p**ockets are your **p**erfect **p**rotection! (Note: Remember it was in Nepal where I first discovered all the locals with their sewing machines on the streets of Kathmandu. I *never* forgot!) To this day, I always have the seamstress near my house sew pockets in the insides of my pants to hide my money.

One memorable occasion was when I was touring with a group. We had half a day free to wander around or we could stay all together for a *five o'clock happy hour.*' I went my separate way and ventured into a Royal Palace. I had the unexpected divine pleasure of meeting the highest ranking monk of the entire country. I sat with a few locals and we had a great discussion and prayers together, with a backdrop of water flowing and soft ancient-echoes music. This was truly my five o'clock

happy hour! When I find myself in moments like this, I prefer to let my mind *melt* into tranquility rather than have my ice *melt* into a drink!

This supreme patriarch, Tep Vong, invited us to come to the Buddha Festival the following day, but I was obligated to rejoin the group, which would be departing for Siem Reap to explore the ruins at Angkor Wat. This was one of those 'Oh, darn' moments when I wish I could have been flexible to wait a day.

Stopping at the Phnom Penh tarantula market, I was introduced to the delicacy of eating sautéed tarantulas in garlic. At first, I was brave enough to eat only one leg, but the sauce was delicious, so I just ate the whole thing. The weirdest sensation was the soft belly on my tongue. Yucky, but yummy! (It reminded me of the delicious fish eyeballs in Taipei.)

CHAPTER 48

"I am not the same, having seen the moon shine
on the other side of the world."
Mary Anne Radmacher

Brunei

Apa kabar!

(How are you?)

Brunei is surrounded by the South China Sea and lies north of Malaysia. The Sultan of Brunei, Hassanal Bolkiah, is one of the world's longest

reigning and few remaining absolute monarchs. I met my tour group at the most amazing hotel I had ever seen; it was dripping with jewels and gold! We toured the country for two days. The most interesting part of the journey occurred when we went to the jungle and saw the proboscis monkeys. Of all the primates, they are the world's most prolific swimmers; they frequently leap from tree limbs above and hit the water with a comical belly flop. Male proboscis monkeys use their fleshy, pendulous noses to attract mates. Scientists think these organs create an echo chamber that amplifies the monkey's call, impressing females and intimidating rival males.

Malaysia

After touring the Golden Sultan's Palace, we boarded the Clipper Odyssey for Sabah, Malaysia. The cruise was the crème de la crème as far as my interests are concerned. We were treated like royalty. The phenomenal crew and staff outnumbered the passengers. For every activity, there was a social director to lead the way. Lanny was in charge of bird watching and observing the endangered orangutans in the wild. Nuby took us snorkeling every other day to find indigenous species of fish, plants, and coral. Boone took the scuba divers to a deeper area for discovering sea magic. Rooster was an anthropologist who took us to five primitive villages within 15 days, where we witnessed horrific, heartbreaking circumcisions of six-year-old boys, an experience too depressing to relate here. But he also took us to tribal dances, marriages, funerals, BBQ feasts, festivals, and we were thrilled to experience plenty of culture shock! We loved Rusty, the piano player from Manila, whose wonderful, enthusiastic spirit kept us happy as we sang and danced during the entire voyage.

Indonesia

We continued to Borneo, Indonesia, where we swam and snorkeled in Jellyfish Lake. This lake is comprised of thousands of jellyfish that are *not* harmful. They have lost their stingers, through the years, due to the fact that they have no predators to defend themselves against. Watching these critters up close and playing with them with our bare hands was almost electrifying! I had also experienced this unbelievable 'jellyfish jubilee' in Palau, next to Guam.

The fifth director, Gretchen, was in charge of taking us to see the dangerous Komodo dragons.

Travel Tip: When taking a photo of yourself with a Komodo dragon, do not stand in front of it even at a distance. It can slither its way to you in an instant with its fatal poisonous spit!

In the next village, we were in for a terrifying shock. We took a bus to a primitive area where our guides had set up an exhibition for us to see. There was a spear-throwing game and a contest among the natives on horses with spears. We watched and cheered as we took pictures of the two teams. After about 40 minutes, one of the men threw his spear into our crowd of spectators and missed my leg by an inch. Was this part of the show? They thought it was funny, so all of them started throwing their spears at us! All of a sudden, our tour guide yelled, "Everybody run...now! Run back to the bus! Hurry! Run fast! We are being attacked!"

We ran for our lives and finally made it inside the bus. The guide was so embarrassed and frightened as well but told us that was a quirk and that it had never happened before. But, it shows you that you can never really be safe, no matter where you go. They had been paid to entertain us. Well, I guess they did!

It reminded me about the story of the little girl trusting and befriending a snake. One day, he bit her. She asked in her last dying breath, "Why? I thought we were friends."

He replied with a wink, "You knew I was a snake when you met me. I am still a snake!"

Yes, there are wild savages out there, and you never know who you can trust.

One of the most memorable surprises on the ship was when the captain told us that we would be crossing the equator at 5:30 a.m. He also announced that if anybody would like to dive off one end of the boat and be picked up minutes later from the other side of the equator, that we should be up and on the bow of the ship at that time. We all said, "No Way." But guess what? Everybody showed up! As we emerged from the sea, all of our directors were there with crowns of stars for everyone to celebrate our achievements!

CHAPTER 49

"I was not born for one corner.
The whole world is my native land."
Seneca

Venezuela

While listening to the news one day, I happened upon the story of Hugo Chavez and his demise on March 3, 2013. It was announced that there was going be a big funeral with festivities to follow in his honor. I immediately sought out the first working flight, with the perk of a paid layover, right into the heart of the action in Caracas and made my way into history (like I did in Berlin when the wall came tumbling down). Hugo Chavez was a popular socialist ruler who rose to power democratically in a 2002 election. It was after a failed attempt at a coup-de-gras in 1992 when he held a high rank in the Venezuelan military. Though the coup proved unsuccessful, his administration of the country, just ten years later, would pan out far better, depending upon which Venezuelan you asked and on which particular day you asked him.

Unfortunately, as years have passed, things have taken a turn for the worse in Venezuela. After the passing of the charismatic leader Chavez, the national economy plummeted. In the ensuing years, the country's once-vast resources have been depleted, and a thrifty shopper would now find nothing but empty shelves in the once-thriving marketplaces of Caracas.

In fact, I realized when I was writing this book that this country was the first of many I explored in 1970! Looking back through my journals, I saw that I actually took five different vacations to five different countries on my own time the very first year of my *independence.* When my other co-workers asked how I could afford to do this, I told them the truth, that I had taken out loans from banks and also a loan from an old high school boyfriend Mac Mc, may he rest in peace. I always paid back my debts when I returned home.

Cuba

Hola chicas!

I had never been to a country on a mission-type trip to help the locals, so this was a first. This Caribbean island is beautiful with its white sandy beaches and colonial architecture. It is famous for its rum, cigars, and salsa. Despite being under communistic rule of Fidel Castro for decades, the Cuban people are lively and cheerful and ready to sing and dance anytime and anywhere. Their kindness and hospitality will steal your heart.

This tour was set up by the organization 'Go Eat Give' to take one for an eye-opening cultural insight. During this particular excursion, led by Sadia from the Dominican Republic, we helped the native farmers with their gardens by pulling weeds, and we even made a game of it to see who could pull the biggest one. We contributed supplies: items that were difficult to purchase. We also volunteered at the mosaic studio of artist Jose Fuster by helping them decorate one of their walls, a blending of colors with little mosaic pieces.

The Cubans were so eager to share their music that they brought their instruments to the beach. We really loved watching everyone smiling, singing, and dancing while enjoying the beach atmosphere.

And, of course, we joined in! And I had to learn another song in Spanish. When I looked out over the waves, there were even people dancing in the water, *living the vida loca*. This was my kind of place!

CHAPTER 50

"Travel makes one modest.
You see what a tiny place you occupy in the world."
Gustave Flaubert

Antarctic Expedition

The Antarctic exploration extended from the end of the nineteenth century to the early 1920s. The continent became the focus of an international effort of scientific and geographical exploration. Sixteen major expeditions were launched from eight different countries. Each exploration became a feat of endurance overcoming major obstacles and costing the lives of 17 explorers. The Antarctic is surrounded by ocean and is made up of icebergs, glaciers, and shelf-ice, and its elevation is 9,300 feet above sea level. Marine mammals include whales, porpoises, and seals, but the class acts are definitely the penguins.

Our journey began in Ushuaia, taking us to Tierra Del Fuego, making our way south through the Drake Passage, then traveling back up toward Penguin Island. Every day, we anchored at a new spot where we disembarked in small zodiac boats to explore different islands. Each one was more exotic than the last, with different species of penguins. Early Antarctic explorers wrongly classified penguins as fish instead of birds. Not only are they birds, they are superbly designed for their job: they can fly underwater with great skill at speeds up to 25 mph.

On dry land, they waddle and hop over rocks, but on snow they can push themselves along on their stomachs. There are 17 species of penguins, but only four breed on the Antarctic continent: the Adelie, the Emperor, the Chinstrap, and the Gentoo. They are insulated with a thick layer of blubber and a dense network of waterproof plumage. Some can reach depths of 1,000 feet or more and stay submerged for up to 25 minutes. Adult pairs take turns incubating their eggs and feeding their chicks. Penguins have more feathers per square inch than any other bird on Earth. They are curious and will come very close to you, but we were instructed not to touch.

> *Note:* If you really have a hankering for touching a penguin, one of the few places to have this encounter is the Ski Dubai exhibit in the United Arab Emirates. It is a perfectly organized and very sanitary sub-zero environment. You are given thermal wear and only allowed to touch after hand-sanitizing. Then you are allowed to gently touch and stroke their penguin feathers. Expert guides teach you

about their natural habitats and behaviors. My daughter, Brigitte, told me about it and beat me to it. I immediately flew a quick layover and scratched it off my bucket list, too!

One of the greatest explorers was Sir Francis Drake, who had been commissioned by Queen Elizabeth I. The body of water he discovered was named the Drake Passage, in his honor. It is one of the most treacherous bodies of water in the world: a 600-mile stretch at the convergence of the Atlantic, Pacific, and Southern Oceans with chaotic and unpredictable violent winds, high waves, and changing currents.

Travel Tip: Do not dance the tango when going through the Drake Passage!

Let me explain. Sherry and I were on a cruise for two weeks, seeing the most fabulous scenery and learning from enriching programs and lectures. However, the night that we had a tango lesson by our six alluring and macho Argentine guides was the exact night that we were sailing through the Drake Passage. No one could even stand up, much less dance. We slid all over the place. It became the DRAKE SHAKE! I think Sir Francis turned over in his grave from watching this chaos!

We finally gave up and went to our beds, which, we discovered, had belts attached to them. We were advised to 'buckle up.' During the night, the passengers who did not fasten their belts before they fell asleep were literally thrown out of their beds. My bed was two feet from Sherry's, and I got thrown out. Of course, Sherry slept through the night and never knew what had happened! Why do I always attract danger?

One of the highlights of the trip occurred when we took pictures from the ship's cockpit. The captain was sharp enough to capture the exact moment when a whale jumped up and then descended back into the ocean. The setting sun caused a blazing fiery orange-gold hue on the magnificent tail of the whale!! It was glorious.

***

So ends my *tales* of my superb amazing adventures: tales of how I almost lost mine *winging it* through seven continents!

This is me...winging it...through seven continents!

EPILOGUE

LIVING THE DREAM

It has been an absolute incredible life of traveling half of this planet. However, there comes a time to give up the back-breaking equation of it and just enjoy doing the other half more leisurely. I don't think I can hang upside down from the overhead rack anymore, so why not give it a break?

So I don't break my back again!

My Ode To Retirees

Almost 50 years ago, I followed my heart
I chose a life emphasizing my art
What better way to see the world, to party and drink brew
Than becoming a glamorous 'airline stew'

Adventures in cultures all over the globe...Italy, Africa, Egypt, Greece
Tango in Argentina...eating French soufflés in Nice
Bargains in India and China, when will this shopping cease?
Riding camels in Dubai to a bar-b-q feast

For China plates, it was England we went
We bought loads of porcelain, wow, the money we spent
In Palau, snorkeling with jellyfish costs a huge fee
We healed with black mud in Israel's Dead Sea

We've all been the masters of 'shop till you drop'
My Korean medicine chest was 'over the top'
The gate agents announce, "no more carry-ons admit"
While the pilots were cramming in our presents to fit!

In France, my friend (Kat) made me wake before six
"Ah merde", a ridiculous hour
So, before our flight back to the USA
We jogged to the Eiffel Tower!

Mai Tais in Hawaii, Piscos in Peru, the wines of 'gay Paree
Brazil's caipirinhas, Hawaii's mai tais, and the beers from Germany
Island piña coladas, Mexico's tequila, saké in Japan
But it's hard to be high... when in the sky, so now, it's time to land

'Jet Recurrent' is finished...no more need to shout:
"Release seat belts"...(duh)..."Get up and get out"
Instead of LAST, we'll be the FIRST when they say,
"Good exit.... leave everything....come this way"
(Persuasive we'll BE..... as we yell, "FOLLOW ME!")

Hard work is now done, what a great sensation
The next time I fly? Delta Dream Vacation!
This amazing company treats you like a star
Taking care of their family, "READY WHEN YOU ARE"

Early birds, jet lag, serving food, coffee, tea
From all of this, it is time to be free
Flying off into the sunset, singing praises of glee
To amazing adventures of A Sky Goddess!...Who Me???

My father memorized and lived by this carpe diem (seize the day) message and taught me to do the same:

Lose the day loitering, 'twill be the same story
To-morrow, and the next more dilatory,
For indecision brings its own delays,
And days are lost lamenting o'er lost days.
Are you in earnest? Seize this very minute!
What you can do, or think you can, begin it!
Only engage, and then the mind grows heated;
Begin it, and the work will be completed
Johann Wolfgang von Goethe

"Those who try to accomplish tasks to follow their dreams
must expect to encounter difficulties.
If I had not climbed the mountain,
I would not have had the chance to glimpse
the vast ocean on the other side."
Dr. Joseph B. Miller

Looking at a world map with my Dad, Dr. Miller

And now, looking for my next rabbit hole...

PHOTO GALLERY

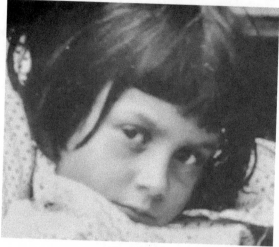

Alice Liddell

Alice Liddell (above) was the little girl, 4 years old, that inspired Lewis Carroll (aka Charles Dodgen) to write Alice in Wonderland, in 1865, and 82 years later I was born and named after her.

Little Alice

My Dad, who named me Alice

Growing up in Sweet Home Alabama family

Fannie, our beloved nanny

Fannie...40 years later

Me and my sister at a costume party

My family

My lifelong friend Sherry

The birds we bred (see page 131)

Chiang Mai, my favorite villlage in Thailand

Lake Louise, Canada

Sandra, my sexiest friend since we were 14 years old.

Krazy Kat

Sandy modeling with me.

Award winner, Casey Grant, who urged me to write my book…As she wrote about Aviation History, I told 'the rest of the story'…Aviation Adventures!

Annabelle Gurwitch and me, two author cousins, wearing the T-shirt dress I made of different countries

Me and Audrey in our favorite uniforms

45 years later with Isabelle in our red signature uniforms

My husband Alain

In Brazil Carnival parade with Marcia

Independence Day!

Pouring coffee with very kind locals in Dubai

Pawberry Punch, a favorite grape drink for kids we used to serve with Dusty, the Air Lion's picture

Lanny Dean, Dr. P. Pack Leader

Norman the Magician

Willie T. Bahamas, Pilot

Ricky Hirsch from the Wet Willie Band

Gregg Allman

Billy Joe Royal and Brenda Hogan

James Brown

Joe Namath
ROLL TIDE!

Willie Nelson

Omar Sharif

Penelope, my friend from Daytona, a bathing suit model

Lying on the floor writing this book (due to back pain), because I worked too hard and played even harder!

THE INSPIRATION

Brad (this book's inspiration) and his family, Wendy, Parker and Brady

CPSIA information can be obtained
at www.ICGtesting.com
Printed in the USA
LVHW041521280820
664252LV00005B/500

9 780996 893343